W9-AMA-930

Brand New Teacher

Carol Keeney

Vested Publishing
Monroe, Connecticut 06468

BRAND NEW TEACHER
by Carol Keeney

Library of Congress Control Number: 2005924547

VESTED PUBLISHING
PO Box 400
Monroe CT 06468

Find us on the web at:
http://www.brandnewteacher.com

NOTICE OF RIGHTS

Copyright © 2006 Vested Publishing All rights reserved. No part of this book may be reproduced or transmitted in any form by any means without the prior written permission of the publisher, except by a reviewer quoting passages.

DISCLAIMER

The contents of this book is distributed on an as-is basis. No warranty is offered or implied. Neither the author nor Vested Publishing shall have any liability in respect to any loss or damage caused or alleged to be caused by the instructions contained in this book

ISBN 0-9752699-0-9

ACKNOWLEDGEMENTS

Special gratitude for reviewing Brand New Teacher goes to Roberta Meier, Lorraine Quinn, Christine Gargano, Judy Lichenstein and Kathy Conroy.

Thank you George B. Abbott for your great drawings and Carol Keeney for the figure art.

Thank you Robert Aulicino for the cover design.

Thank you Beth Bruno for proof reading and editorial assistance.

Dedication

This book is dedicated to my husband who encouraged me to share my thoughts on teaching and helped me to make this book a reality. To my sons who I hope will be encouraged by this book to always follow their dreams and desires. To my parents who were always there for me. To my students who taught me so much.

" So, OTHER THAN THAT, HOW WAS YOUR
    FIRST DAY AS A TEACHER? "

Table of Contents

Tables

Stories and Rhymes

Introduction

As a new teacher, your administration will expect you to be a quick study. Based on your education and common sense it will be concluded that you know how to teach. However, teaching certification and readiness are not always the same. College methods classes don't always prepare students for the day-to-day challenges of the classroom. This book will close that gap so that you feel and look more experienced. Parents will feel confident to bring their children to your early grade classroom or day-care program.

This book is an easy read. You will not have to struggle through heavy philosophy. I will walk you through it all. Because Brand New Teacher is presented as a theatrical metaphor, ideas come to life. Picture yourself as an actor, director or musical conductor blending classroom management and teaching techniques into an enthusiastic learning environment.

The book is organized into four sections

Part One   In this section, you learn the vital link between teaching and acting. This section will help you develop your teaching persona. You will be able to teach and reach your students! You will project your lessons enthusiastically, and you will instruct your students effectively! In the first chapter you are encouraged to examine self development through assertive training, affirmations and relaxation. Development in this area is a prelude to learning acting in Chapter Two.

Part Two   This section illustrates the importance of organization in the classroom. You will learn how to transform a group of students into a class community; you will learn the steps to recognize every student early-on. You will be given suggestions for setting up furniture that will change the space effectively in your classroom. You will learn design to create a sense of clarity. All of this will be shown with illustrations. Just follow the steps.

Part Three This sections helps you add specific props to your set (classroom) to instill curiosity into students' minds. This will encourage students to take part in learning. Create a print-rich environment by following simple ideas. Look at Math as the fun and creative subject it can be! Learn initial lessons and activities that will grab your students' attention. If you need a generic Art lesson as a follow-up, you have a set of them to choose from. No need to hunt and peck for ideas—they are all in this book!

Part Four Every actor needs his lines. The chapters in this section give you the timed lines and lessons to perform during your first week; or, whatever week you choose to start. These lessons address all subject areas and teach you a multi-disciplinary approach. You will use the senses to vary your approaches.

You will be given transitional tips that could take years of experience to collect. Use these ideas to build lessons and activities for the rest of the year. It will work!

I have developed questions from various picture books that will move you beyond the initial knowledge question in shared reading activities. You won't have to wonder what to do or say next because it is all here.

Take the worry out of dealing with common behavior problems. I tell you what to do—and what to do if it doesn't work.

After reading this book, you will adapt what has worked for you. Add these resources to your repertoire and become the teacher you hoped you would be!

Carol Keeney

Self Empowerment

Comprehension: Use the questions below as an aid to reinforce comprehension of the chapters.

The Main Character

Why is appearance a key factor in teaching?

Why is listening an important skill in teaching?

Name two reasons for using assertiveness in the classroom?

Name three methods for diffusing a behavior problem?

What is the difference between assertiveness and aggressiveness?

What does it mean to desire to be assertive?

Can the quiz questions in Assertive Techniques be used to make-up your own affirmations?

The Actor in You

How can acting lessons raise your teaching ability above the average?

Can the new role you play in the classroom become part of you? Will it be natural for you to play it?

Which of the following is the study of "action" and "movement?" (a) voice (b)pantomine (c) Facial Fun

What does concentration have to do with acting?

Do I have to choose a role model other than myself?

What does the formula LET=E mean?

Do I have to learn everything before I act in the classroom?

The Main character

"To increase your influence,
you must become what we call an assertive teacher"

—Lee Canter

A main character is the ultimate voice in a production. The main character works in tandem with the other characters, not alone. If the play is not a monologue, the main character communicates with the other characters, bringing their roles to life. You, the teacher, will be the director who works with all the other actors, the students, to bring out the best in each of them. Ultimately, you will be able to step back and allow these main characters to take center stage, but only when they have learned to be responsively engaged in the learning process.

You will start to set the stage for a realistic learning environment by your own presentation. Your **appearance** will be a key factor because your students will decide early on whether or not you are truly a leader. You might say, "But I am not even sure they will listen to me!" Don't worry, many of us felt that way at first. Remember, I said your appearance is the key, not your inner voice. How good an actor are you? Your goal is to convince your audience that you have been teaching for years. Your appearance will be an important factor in the impression you give to your students. Remember that appropriate costumes help to set the stage for any production. Your clothes do not have to be fancy or expensive but it will be beneficial to wear clothes that do not scream to be noticed. Skimpy clothes or exotic prints will focus the children on style, but will draw their attention away from the subject at hand. Even if you look great in those clothes, remember, that isn't the goal. Tone it down to look the part of the main character you are playing.

Bank of Memories

Believe it or not, you have a bank of memories in your past from which you can draw. You are not a person who has been living in a vacuum up until now. So I will ask you to recall a time when you dealt with children successfully. Maybe you baby sat or maybe you have been a counselor. Maybe you are a parent. How did you manage to get the attention of your audience? How did you keep their attention? What types of situations were challenging? How did you meet those challenges? By examining these past experiences you can boost your self confidence and this will help you face new challenges in the classroom. Use the next page to begin exploring some of your memories of guiding children. This exercise is helpful, consider starting a **personal journal** in which you can record your journey into teaching.

Fewer Words Say More

When I began teaching I pictured a long day that had to be filled by hundreds of words spoken by me. What was I going to say first, and then what, and how was I going to fill the day with enough words? I found out that even though you speak enough to be thirsty, fewer words are clearer and more powerful. Think of friends who tell of an incident that happened at 3 o'clock and begin their story with what they had for breakfast. We've all known someone like that. When they get to the punch line we really don't care what happened, do we? The bottom line is that fewer words say more. Practice communicating with your friends using fewer words. Think a little more before you speak and **choose your words** carefully. Don't go off on a tangent telling another story inside the main story. Stick to the point. It will take practice because we usually do not monitor our own speech, but it is an interesting exercise and one that will probably be appreciated by the listener.

As you get to know your class, you will begin to feel more familiar with them. Don't fall into the trap of talking to your students as if they

Personal Journal

List situations below that involved interaction between you and a child:.

List challenges that resulted from these interactions:

How did you overcome these challenges?

are neighbors. It is important to keep the relationship professional. This doesn't mean that you can't enjoy an activity with them, but you need to keep the activity on track. If you had a bad day because your son could not find his sneaker or you couldn't start your car, deal with those feelings before you go into the classroom. When I was in the first grade we didn't think the teachers ate. That might have been too extreme an impression, but there does need to be a clear delineation of roles. You are the teacher, you are the leader and you are ultimately the one in control.

A Personal Note

I recently met a young woman whom I had taught in the first grade. She reminded me that when she was my new student she had also been a new immigrant from Italy. She spoke a limited amount of English at the time and was natually apprehensive about beginning in a public school in New York. I remembered her. She had been shy and seemingly insecure but interested in this new and shiny place that was to be her classroom. I remember the day she entered the room with her mom and the school secretary. She had started a school a few weeks after opening day. I remember stooping down to her level and looking at her eye to eye. In a quiet way I tried to welcome her and reassure her that all would be well. Now, meeting her two decades later, she complimented me for the way I had treated her. She said that she remembered that I had admired her red shoes. She said that my kind words and patience had made all the difference to her adjustment to school.

You are the Ultimate Voice

Think back to all the people who have taught you in your life. Take a few minutes to reflect on their personalities and teaching styles. Think about the ones who were the most **effective teachers**. You will discover that many of them were instinctively assertive or had taken assertiveness training.

Lee Canter is considered to be the father of assertive discipline. His original text *Assertive Discipline: A Take Charge Approach for Today's Educator* was written over twenty-years ago and he makes the following suggestions for setting up a behavior plan: 1) that students be taught responsible behavior within the community of the classroom and ulti-

mately responsible behavior within the community of the classroom and ultimately, the school, 2) expectations need to be discussed, 3) a few simple
positive and observable rules need to be decided upon, 4) praise is para-
mount as a motivating factor and, 5) any consequences needs to be a healthy
one; no physical or emotional abuse can be used.

In setting up a behavior plan go in with a good attitude. Tell the children,
"You can do this!" Set-up a calendar in the
back of each child's notebook. At the end of
each day, stamp the chart for good **behavior**;
you can use a happy-face stamp. A question
mark can indicate a warning. Three warn-
ings can equal one phone call home.

**Lee Canter &
Associates
1275 Coral Tree Place
Los Angeles 90066**

Handle the phone call tactfully. Introduce yourself and mention something positive about the child's behavior. Follow with the punch-line: "He
seems to be having problems staying on task or following direction." Get
the parents on the team; it means everything to the child's success.

If you come across more serious behavior problems, you need to ask your
school administration for help and set-up a specific behavior contract with
this student. He will need to work on one specific behavior problem at a
time, and be consistently praised and rewarded for positive efforts.

Assertiveness programs and resources can be obtained from Lee Canter
& Associates.

Assertive Techniques

Consider assertive techniques as a framework for your teaching style. I
learned a great deal about assertiveness by participating in seminars, where
we practiced how to solve communication problems through assertive
techniques.

In place of compliant behavior that caused us not to confront a problem or anger that caused us to destroy any communication, we learned to
truly **listen** to people. We have all heard the pat statement, "I hear you",
but how many people really do hear what someone else is trying to say?
I think the ability to allow someone to be heard is a gift some people are
just not willing to give. Sometimes we only want to be heard ourselves
and when that doesn't work we repeat our ideas even louder. With assertive techniques you can allow that person to be heard, acknowledge what
he is saying by putting his thoughts in your own words and then calmly
stating whether you agree with his ideas or whether you have another
idea. The point is that you need to diffuse the situation, it helps to be
able to calm the situation before it spirals out of control. If you listen

calmly to what is going on and verbally referee the situation you will not only be able to recover the learning environment, you will also gain more respect from your students. If Johnny refuses to follow a clear direction you may become **angry** because you are fearful the situation may escalate out of control. The tendency might be to raise your voice and shout out the direction. This creates exactly what you don't want, a power play.

How to diffuse a situation

Ask Johnny why he is having a problem conforming to the request?

Echo-back to Johnny what he said. Echoing back will allow you to get to know Johnny's feelings. Johnny will sense that you sincerely wish to understand him. He will be reassured that you are listening to him when he hears his concerns echoed back to him.

Offer a solution, if available and then calmly repeat the request if it is appropriate to do so. Many times Johnny will conform because a meeting of the minds has occurred. Guaranteed you have gained some respect form Johnny because you were not too intimidated to hear him.

Please do not confuse the two words assertiveness and aggressiveness. **Assertiveness** comes from the core of confidence and **self respect**. It is from this secure stance that you can deal with conflict successfully. You see, if we truly listen to others, we can resolve the situation from there. As a brand new teacher, don't be threatened by conflict. Conflict is part of life and occurs in every classroom. See chapter 13, *Conflicts on the Set* for more information.

Simple quiz

Try this simple quiz to text your assertiveness. Check T(rue) or F(alse) for each of the following

	T	F
I am not responsible for the behavior of others	☐	☐
I do not change my mind when challenged by others	☐	☐
Most of the time I have a clear idea of what I expect from others	☐	☐
I make clear statements about what I want and need from others	☐	☐
I find it easy to say no to someone if it is in my best interest	☐	☐
I never react to anger with anger	☐	☐
I never raise my voice even when I know I am right	☐	☐
I am always willing to confront strong minded individuals	☐	☐
I don't have to be overly confident to act assertively	☐	☐
I don't have to be born assertive; assertiveness can be developed	☐	☐
I welcome debate with strong minded individuals	☐	☐
I handle criticism easily and it doesn't bother me that much	☐	☐

Total:

If you scored **eight points or less** ...
in the T(rue) column, you have room to grow as an assertive person. You can do this by getting on the road to change.

- ▼ Keep this book on your night stand and read *Desire to be Assertive* and *Affirming to be Assertive* every night (see below).
- ▸ See the bibliography for book and internet resources
- ▸ Check out Lee Canter's web site at http://www.canter.net
- ▸ Observe other teachers who have these skills.

Desire to be Assertive

Adjust your attitude: Remember your right to respect is valuable. You are important and deserve respect. You will receive it in direct proportion to how much you truly believe you deserve it. Remember to keep these three ideas in mind; assertiveness works when you embrace them:

You have the right to be heard in the classroom. You are not on a TV channel that can be ignored or changed.

Children are people who deserve respect too. Don't be afraid to set up positive rules and guideline in the classroom. Many children feel more secure in a structured setting because they know what they can expect from you.

Don't hesitate to set-up an environment that will work for everyone. This environment will expand and change throughout the year but the very foundation that you will build as a brand new teacher will set the stage for a successful school year. This book will help you build that strong foundation.

Affirming to be Assertive

Sit alone in a quiet spot at home. Choose one of the affirmations listed below or write one of your own; look at the quiz for ideas. Remember to keep the statement positive and write the sentence in the present tense as if it is already true. Don't write, "I hope I do well in the classroom and the children listen to me."

Write your statement seven times, noticing if oppositional thoughts enter your mind. If they do, jot them on the margin of your paper. As you continue these exercises each day for a number of days, notice how negative thoughts decrease as you start to believe your positive statement.

"I really speak at a moderate pace, slowly and clearly."

"I present myself as a confident teacher."

"I am always properly prepared for my school day."

A Personal Note

Congratulations! You have done well and now you are about to embark on a new and challenging career. I wish you all the best! I remember the beginning of my career well. I remember how proud I was to say that I was a brand new teacher. I had reached my goal and I couldn't wait to save the world. I thought a lot about myself and my abilities. I had always studied hard and done fairly well in my classes. I felt I was a kind person and would easily be able to help any student achieve his goals, especially in the first grade. I am embarassed to admit to you that I didn't do too well that first year. I would say that my main problem at the time was inexperience. I meant well, but I just didn't know how to organize my classroom and my day. Did I ask for suggestions? Sure I did. Did I try some worthwhile ideas? Yes again. I tried so many ideas that the class didn't know what to expect from me. Truthfully, the feeling of uncertainly was mutual. How I wished for the type of book you are now holding: one that address aspects of organization, concept building, behavior issues, transitional tips, art projects and actual dialogue to walk down that first road. Hopefully, you will think of this handbook as my voice calmly guiding you through your first experience as a brand new teacher. You'll be great!

"HOW'RE YOU FIXED FOR EXCITEMENT?"

The Actor in You

Good teaching is one-fourth preparation and three-fourths theater.

-- Gail Godwin

Decades ago, "Psycho Cybernetics" was written by Maxwell Maltz, MD. The book held that we could achieve whatever we wanted through belief. It was a radical idea at the time, yet it caught on and many books followed with the same idea. Books such as The *Magic of Believing* by Bristol and *The Power of Positive Thinking* by Dr. Norman Vincent Peale showed how affirmations can influence our belief system through the subconscious mind. The theme was and is: If you only have faith in yourself, anything is possible!

Acting, though less publicized, affects belief systems, too. With acting lessons, people have not only increased their **self-confidence** but also their awareness and observation skills, too. In addition, the positive personality changes appear to be automatic, and this is exciting news. Go on the Internet and you'll find case studies of people who have taken acting lessons for one purpose, and to their amazement, improved their self image immediately. In some instances, acting students were not aware of their positive personality traits until it was brought to their attention by a friend or family member.

Acting is a creative outlet too.

Teaching and Acting

There is a scholarly connection between teaching and acting supported by the work of Robert T. Tauber and Cathy Sargent of the Behrend College at Penn State University. I wish to draw from their book entitled *Acting for Teachers: Using Performance skills in the classroom* a partial reprint from a testimonial (Appendix II) by Professor Raymond J. Clough, Department of Modern Languages, Canisius College:

> Clough relates an incident he had when he went to hear Vincent Price do a dramatic reading of Edgar Allan Poe's The *Tell-Tale Heart*. Clough says, "…. Price held his audience spell bound for the entire reading. **He used all the tricks of his trade** – dramatic pauses, voice modulation and projection, crisp articulation. He scanned the audience, seemed to be speaking to each one of us. **The effect was verbal alchemy**…."

Imagine the power of these skills in the hands of a teacher – the use of dramatic pauses, voice modulation and projection in front of a K to 2 class. Imagine how it would improve the chemistry in your classroom.

Acting Demystified

You don't have to get a university degree in drama to learn how to act. There is no hidden secret to gaining these skills. In order to act, you need to follow a plan that includes study, concentration and practice. Specifically, you will have to do the following:

1) Study the role you will play
2) Concentrate on the role when you perform it in front of your class.

If you believe in children and feel benevolent toward them, **the best role to play is *yourself.*** You'll see your teaching skills zoom to new heights after practicing and applying the exercises in this chapter. If you would rather use another teacher as a role model, see the section *Choosing an External Role Model*.

Voice Exercises

The exercises below will help you focus on yourself and be objective. After you have practiced these exercises try some of the other exercises in Chapter 11; imagine how you would apply what you have practiced.

Practice modulating your voice.

Look at *This Old Man.* on page 114.

- Say it into a tape recorder as you would in front of a class.

- Practice changing the pitch of your voice on certain words for emphasis. Lower your voice to a whisper to change the emphasis on other key words.

- Practice until satisfied and say the new version into the tape recorder.

Practice your rate of speech.

Use *This Old Man*

- Practice changing your speaking rate from slower on some words and faster on others

- Say the new version into the tape recorder when you are satisfied with your practice.

Practice changing voice

Look at a *Short Vowel Story* on p 106

- Say it into a tape recorder like you would in front of a class.

- Practice speaking in each characters' voice.

- Say the new version into a tape recorder.

TIME OUT

Storytelling can come alive as a theatrical event when you read the words of various characters in unique voices. Try watching some fun movies and listen to the **voice-overs** done by actors. *Three Little Pigs* is a good fairy tale to use to practice voice changes.

Practice using a mirror

For this exercise use a hand-held mirror.

- Look at your reflection and practice saying the long vowel sounds *A E I O U.*

- Repeat these exercises three times

🖐 TIME OUT

You can recite simple nursery rhymes while looking in the mirror. You will need to be familiar with these verses as an early grade teacher. The sing-song quality of rhyming words are a wonderful introduction to reading and word families. Say these nursery rhymes slowly as each exercise will help you to **enunciate your words** and to **speak at a moderate leve**l. Good presentation skills are a necessary tool for keeping the attention of your class!

Pantomine and Voice

These execises are designed to be done silently in your mind. The emphasis is on **action** and **movement**.

Practice a fire drill

Pretend you must move your class out of the room quickly.

- What hand movements will you use with the children?

- How will you walk around the classroom?

- How will your voice modulate when giving instructions?

📄   NOTE: IN YOUR MIND, IMAGINE THAT THE TABLES ARE NUMBERED BY ROWS. TEACH EACH GROUP IN TURN TO JOIN THE LINE SILENTLY WHEN YOU SIGNAL IT IS THEIR TURN. IMAGINE BREAKING DOWN THIS WHOLE PROCEDURE INTO SIMPLE SENTENCES SUGGESTED BY THE CHILDREN. PRETEND YOU ARE WRITING THESE SENTENCES ON A CHART FOR FUTURE REFERENCE.

A Generic situation

Pretend you must distribute pencils for any given lesson

- The same questions apply as in the fire drill above. Before you begin, think how you might do this.

📄   INSTEAD OF HANDING OUT ONE PENCIL TO EACH CHILD, TRY GIVING A SET OF PENCILS TO FOUR CHILDREN. THESE CHILDREN CAN THEN GIVE OUT THE PENCILS TO NEARBY GROUPS.

Practice Reading a picture book

If your thinking, "that's too easy," think again!

📄   YOU MAY NOT HAVE MASTERED READING UPSIDE DOWN YET. READ A BOOK WITH THE WORDS FACING YOU AS YOU SIT IN A CHAIR. NOW, TURN THE BOOK AROUND AND SLOWLY MOVE IT IN A CIRCULAR MOTION SO THAT ALL THE CHILDREN CAN GLANCE AT THE PICTURES. BE CAREFUL NOT TO BLOCK THE TEXT WITH YOUR FINGERS AS YOU SHOW THE PICTURES.

🖐 **Time Out**

Acting is not a static process, it is dynamic, too. You must be able to **concentrate** on voice, movement and facial expressions simultaneously in order for acting to work. These exercises sharpen that ablity.

Knowing where you are going is equally important as concentration. The **Pantomine and Voice** exercises encourage you to plan—or stage what you will be doing in the classroom. By asking questions and mentally rehearsing different activities, you are **staging** and **scripting** your performance. This will allow you to anticipate various management situations.

Use the activites and scripts in this book for your rehearsals.

Facial Fun

A WAY TO IMPACT A CHILD'S CONFIDENCE AND MOTIVATION.

Professional Look

Look into the mirror and try on some faces. What you are looking for is the *In Charge* look. You may have just stepped in front of the class but you are the leader. Don't be surprised if you make yourself laugh a few times before you find your face looking more serious and determined.

Surprised Look

Practice the expression of *Happily Surprised* for a child who has done something well. You will find children watching your face to read their success or failure. This expression can be used as an importan motivator.

Disappointed Look

Look at yourself in the mirror eye to eye. Now change your expression to portray a *little disappointment*. In the mirror, act as if you have proposed a set of choices for this child and he is willing to cooperate with you—now, change your expression to a *pleasant* one.

🖐 **Time Out**

Have you ever heard the saying regarding someone's skill, "He makes it look easy." There was probably a lot of practice involved behind the scenes to make whatever he did, look easy. The exercises in this chapter are easy to do by yourself but you will have to practice them to make it look easy and feel natural in the classroom.

My suggestion is not to try to do it all at once, in one week or in one month. Instead, take each exercise and become comfortable with it. Try it in the classroom, and then come back and focus on another skill.

Perfection is not the goal with these exercises. If something did not work out the way you expected it to in the classroom, it will next time.

When Gene Hackman starred in *The Firm*, he had to do a scuba diving scene. The actor turned to professional scuba diver Daniel Lenihan to study the role. Hackman learned enough from Lenihan to make movie fans believe he had been scuba diving all his life.

Choosing an external role

Identifying the role of an effective teacher is the first step in actually becoming an effective teacher. Think back to your childhood; is there a teacher you admired? Did you feel that you and your classmates vied for this teacher's attention? Did you feel **enthusiastic** toward lessons presented to you? Did you feel that this teacher respected you as a person?

Consider for a moment that this teacher had certain attributes that contributed to his or her popularity: This teacher probably liked children. This teacher enjoyed their spontaneity, and was careful not to take that spontaneity away from them. This teacher probably enjoyed treating children like little adults too.

A **natural result** of this kind of attitude toward children is **enthusiasm**.

Since these attributes are common to highly successful teachers, lets put them into a formula for easy recall.

L= like children
E=Enjoy the spontaneity of children
T=Treat them like adults

Now, lets factor in enthusiasm as the result.

LET = Enthusiasm

By Applying this formula LET = E to any role you choose to play, you are on your way to becoming a effective teacher.

How to use the formula

Unless you have a LET inspired teacher in mind, follow the steps below:
1. Make-up an imaginary teacher, or think of one from the past.
2. Grab this image! Don't wait for perfection.
3. Make-believe that this image is a LET inspired teacher.
4. Imagine you have become this imaginary teacher.
5. Concentrate on your new role as you read and re-read this book.

Role Play Exercises
USE CONFLICTS ON THE SET FROM CHAPTER 13.

Practice changing viewpoints
Repeat this exercise for each one of the characters in *Conflicts on the Set.*

◄ Read Scenes starting with the first character Leo Lost into a tape recorder and note any annoyance or other feelings in yourself.

◄ Imagine playing the role of a LET inspired teacher

◄ When you feel comfortable with the role, repeat the scene into the tape recorder.

◄ Listen for differences in your voice such as the rate of speed and pitch between the first and second recording. (See voice exercises on the previous page for help doing this). The confidence protrayed through your voice will have a direct impact on your effectiveness.

Experimenting
Repeat the exercises using the *Looks* skills from *Facial Fun*

◄ Starting with Leo Lost, practice a *Professional* look, *Surprised* look and *Disappointed* look on your face. Read the scene while practicing each 'Look' into the tape recorder. You should have three recordings when you are finished.

◄ Next, believe the LET inspired teacher is you!. Read the scene into the recorder with a new *Look* on your face. Do this while simultaneously focusing on LET.

◄ Listen to the recordings to determine differences in your speech patterns.

🖐 **Time Out**
I suggested you use *Conflicts on the Set* to practice with LET in the Role Play above. I used this chapter because it might help you sense a dichotomy between the role you now play and that of a LET inspired teacher.

If you sensed some resistance, you know you have a lot of practice ahead of you. Therefore, I recommend that you scavenge this book for every activity you can find and practice doing it as a LET inspired teacher would do it.

If you put this into practice, there will be a rainbow at the end of the tunnel and a time where little or no practice is required by you to perform as a real teacher would.

The Process

Just to make sure we are on the same page, here is an example of the process you'll use. Suppose I asked you to walk, talk and chew gum like Elvis Presley would. To perform that role, you would follow a routine like the following:

- Stage it: First break it down into manageable activities. Walking, talking and chewing gum are 3 distinct activities (See the fire drill on page 24).

- Use pantomime: Practice walking like Elvis would (See Panomine on page 24).

- Use voice exercises: Practice talking like Elvis would (See Voice exercises on page 23).

- Use Facial Expression exercises: Practice chewing gum like Elvis would (See Facial Fun on page 25).

- Concentration: First, Practice walking and talking at the same time. Second, Practice walking, talking and chewing gum at the same time.t.

- Practice: Finally, you would practice and practice until you felt comfortable being Elvis.

Q & A

I am confused as to whether or not I should choose an external role to play or myself.
If you naturally like and enjoy of children (as outlined in the LET formula on page 26), you don't need an extenal role model. Do the voice, pantomine and facial fun exercises and you'll do fine.

After I have practiced these exercises, what should I do next?
Go to Day One, Day Two ....etc., in the Week of Scripts chapter. Practice the daily activities using the skills you acquired in this chapter.

When should I start acting in the classroom?
Immediately! As soon as you practice anything in this chapter, try it in the classroom. Seeing how easy it is and how much fun it is will motivate you to learn and try out more techniques. Your confidence will increase.

Will it become natural so I don't have to practice again?
What you do over and over again will become part of you—just like an athlete. You will not want to discard skills that work well for you.

Personal Note

I had been a teacher for a number of years, when I first visited Universal Studios with my husband. We both volunteered to take part in a comedy skit; it sounded like fun! After just a short time rehearsing our lines, we dressed up and presented the scene to a live audience. The acting was new and exciting for me but somehow familiar. I realized that I acted many times before in the classroom!

After that experience, I viewed my school day from a different focal point. I noticed the similarity between teaching skills and acting skills. Producing a lesson, directing a class or scripting units of study, I was engaged in theatre. This experience empowered me to reach my students and keep them engaged in the process! Each class brought a new dynamic to the show. Over time, I collected many valuable ideas! I have written this book to motivate you and to equip you so that your first year will be only the first of many fun and exciting years of teaching young children!

" Boy! I have just enough education to know that I don't have enough education.

$Part$ **2**

Organization

Comprehension: Use the questions below as an aid to reinforce comprehension of the chapters.

Building a Cohesive Set

📧 Name three reasons why childrens names are important to your success?

📧 Name three ways a Class List can be used?

📧 How can classroom management and empowerment of children be the same thing?

📧 What does "full ownership" of the classroom mean?

Functioning Classroom

📧 Name two ways the seating arrangement in a classroom can be set-up?

📧 What is the drawback of starting with a small group?

📧 Why should you write a letter-to-the-parents in the beginning of school?

📧 What items should you have on hand even before the children bring their own supplies to the classroom?

Readiness

📧 What is the purpose of a Library Center?

In *Brand New Teacher* what chapter can you use as a resource for starting a book list, and as an introduction to reading and thinking skills?

📧 Why use an index file?

📧 Explain the importance of excitement in the motivation of learning?

📧 How do the senses enter into reading?

📧 How do transitional activities and learning games influence the teaching of reading?

Setting the Scene

📧 Why is the appearance of the classroom important to the childrens mood?

📧 What four characteristics of design can we use in the classroom?

📧 Color belongs to one design elements below. Which one?
(a) contrast (b) alignment
(c) proximity (d) repetition

📧 Why is planning on paper important before setting-up your classroom?

📧 Looking at the Classroom Map in the chapter Functioning Classroom how you would set-up your room.?

3

Building a cohesive set

Three things in human life are important: The first is to be kind. The second is to be kind. The third is to be kind.

—Henry James

The Theatre Gazette

Last night the play, "Its All Part of a Days Pay" failed to open. Ticket holders will be given a Credit to a future theatre performance. The producer announced that the actors just could not work together. The director was seen running out of the theatre in a fit of frustration. One of the lead actors explained the problem simply. Everyone was acting as if the play was a one man show. The actors paid no attention to the director or to the needs of their fellow actors. The public is questioning how the director was chosen since he was not able to bring the actors together...

Children need to feel like they are part of the larger community which is their classroom. They need to feel pride in their room and in the family of children who make up their class.

They need to take a part in discussing and creating a set of positive guidelines which will help the classroom run smoothly on a daily basis. They must know that each of them is a key player in setting the tone of the classroom. Building a sense of personal pride and importance in each student is vital to a working classroom set. A classroom set is much like a theatrical production. How many times have you heard about how a particular cast of characters who worked well together or floundered because some actors were not as responsible as others?

Acknowledgement is the key

Do you remember the children's TV show called Romper Room? At the end of each show the teacher would look through a magic mirror and name the children that she pretended to see. Think of how many children's eyes were glued to their TV sets hoping to hear their names. Maybe you were one of those people who enjoyed being singled out on TV. It made you feel special. Acknowledgement is the key.

It will be your responsibility to learn the names of your students as soon as possible. To help you remember the **children's names**, here are a few tips: Try to associate each child with another person you might know who shares this first name. Try noticing how well a child's name seems to suit him. Some names will simply have to be memorized through repeated use. As you take attendance, and as you call on individuals, always use their name. Make up a seating chart and keep it in plain view so you can remind yourself who's who. Draw a diagram of your seating arrangement and make a few copies for future seating changes. See Chapter 4 for information about seating arrangements.

You will need to record your students' names in a number of places at the beginning of the school year. Prepare for that first day before your class arrives by using a **checklist** (See Figure 3-1 next page). From the checklist, you will be able to create labels, name plaques and find many other uses for it.

Class List		
Name	Address	Telephone Number

Figure 3-1
Class List

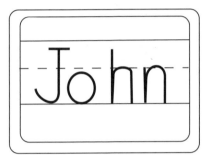

Figure 3-2
Name Plaque

Make Labels from a Class List

1.   Make a class list with space left for information. You will need copies of this list for various teachers and school personnel during the year.

2.   Make a set of name tags that you can use for the first day of school. Print each first-name clearly, capitalizing only the first letter.

3.   Make a set of name labels for hooks in the coat closet. Assigning each child a hook helps them to feel some ownership in the classroom setting.

4.   Make a class list in the back of your plan book. Make sure to record addresses and pertinent phone numbers.

5.   Prepare a stack of index cards by writing one name on each card. These can be kept on the top of your desk in a recipe box and can be used to jot down information about the child's progress. These cards also come in handy for parent-teacher conferences

6.   Make **name plaques** for each desk. This will help your students feel a sense of belonging and will also serve as a model for practicing writing their names (See Figure 3-2 above).

A good way to make children feel like they are part of a team is to allow them to take part in **classroom management**. You can do this by assigning tasks for volunteers to do on a regular basis

empower
class
leaders

Figure 3-3
Monitor Chart

◀

Fasten an envelope and keep blank paper in it for new names.

Naturally, you will not have enough jobs to offer the children at the start of the school year. Take some time to know your students and when you feel they are ready to take on a little responsibility, give a group lesson about a particular job. A good way to make children feel like they are part of a team is to allow them to take part in classroom management. You can do this by assigning tasks for **volunteers** to do on a regular basis. Naturally, you will not have enough jobs to offer the children at the start of the school year. Take some time to know your students and when you feel they are ready to take on a little responsibility, give a group lesson about a particular job. When I say the word job, I am not talking about major maintenance but I am suggesting they assist you with such responsibilities as distributing paper or watering plants. Simplify each step that must be taken and write a simple list of these steps on a chart for referral later on.

By reviewing this chart from time to time, you are teaching your students that words are useful—they record information. Believe it or not we are not born with this reading and writing connection. This connection is made when the readers notice **how words work** on a daily basis. They can see a spoken sentence recorded word by word. They can watch how words can be removed as sentences are reviewed. Finally they can make the connection that each spoken word can be formed as a written word. With a little planning and whole lot of patience you will be transforming little children into a cohesive set of learners and you are their brand new teacher.

Choose a number of Art projects early in the year that can help the children celebrate their **uniqueness** and get to know their classmates on a first name basis.

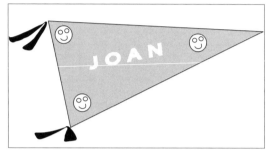

Figure 3-4
Name Banner

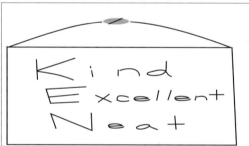

Figure 3-5
Acrostic Poem

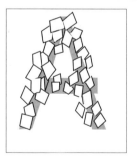

Figure 3-6
Initial Collages

Name Banner

A banner can be made in the form of a pendant or in the shape of a large rectangle. You can use this to celebrate the children's names or to make a team banner. You can also cut out pictures of things the children like and glue them under their names on a large piece of paper. You can add a photo of each child too (See Figure 3-4).

MATERIALS: Prepare a banner for each child by cutting out triangles from colored construction paper.

PROCEDURE: Assuming that the children are about six-years old, I suggest you write each name on a banner using a light-colored highlighter. Print each name carefully using one capital letter and all the rest lowercase. This will serve as a model the children can trace with a crayon. They then can freely decorate their banners by drawing simple pictures and shapes.

THAT EXTRA TOUCH: consider letting the children use seasonal stickers or streamers to decorate their banners.

Acrostic Poem

MATERIALS: This poem can be created from a piece of construction paper cut in the shape of a narrow and long and long rectangle. This project works well if you have help from volunteers in the classroom, or if you work on this project after the children have a better grasp of phonics. It calls for the children to write an adjective describing themselves for each letter of their first name See Figure 3-5).

PROCEDURE: The children receive a paper with the letters of their first names written in caps vertically on the paper. Explain that we usually write from left to right but today we will write from top to the bottom of the paper because we are going to write a poem. Ask them if anyone knows a poem. Share a few simple poems with them. Relate how they will be able to tell readers a little more about themselves with the Acrostic Poem. Frame each one and display them for one of your parent-teacher events. The parents will love reading them. Celebrate these poems by reading a few each day. This is another way of validating student work, and that is so important!.

Initial Collages

MATERIALS: Give the children a piece of construction paper. Prepare these papers before the lesson by writing one large capital on each one representing each child's first name. These letters should take-up most of the width and length of the paper. Also, prepare many colorful squares cut from tissue paper. Distribute white glue to the children at the start of the activity. Remember to pre-teach the children how to use the glue. If you just hand out the glue bottles without instructions a few might squeeze puddles on their paper. It can get ugly! (See Figure 3-6)

PROCEDURE: Practice awareness of each child's initial by allowing them to tell their names and the first letter of their first names. After a clear explanation, allow children time to glue the colored squares on top of their initial. The finished products can be displayed nicely on a bulletin board with their photographs. This activity will help celebrate each student's identity. Use a title such as "Alphabet Art" on the bulletin board to draw attention to their creations.

Personal Note

Early in my career, I was assigned to teach in a run-down public school. As I walked into my classroom, I noticed that there was a concrete block missing in the wall and it had yet to be repaired. The sight of it was depressing to me and I imagined how the children would be affected by the sight on their first day of school. I decided to change that hole into a window box. I took brown construction paper, folded it into a rectangular box and taped it across the bottom half of the hole. Next, I filled the box with multi-colored tissue-paper flowers. The children loved it and began to take pride in their classroom and entrance early on.

You will want your students to feel ownership in their classroom. You will want them to feel good about being part of a clean, organized and exciting environment. An attractive backdrop is essential to this goal. You are lucky to have found this book! It will take the guesswork out of setting-up your bulletin boards. Your students will appreciate it as learners. Adults will be impressed with your know-how as a brand new teacher. You'll be great!

4

Functioning classroom

"Home is where one starts from."

–T.S. Eliot

I n any play, the actors must have directions on where and how they should enter and exit the set. Common sense tells us that if these directions are not followed, the actors will be crashing into each other instead of moving fluidly through the story line. Your classroom will be filled with a large cast. The **furniture** that you use for your classroom must be set up in such a way that the children can function effectively. I would suggest that you keep things simple for the first several weeks. It is important that you keep things consistent at this time so that the children know what to expect when they enter the classroom in the morning. They will feel more secure when have a sense of belonging. So take some time to set up the furniture so that you do not have to change the set for a while.

Ask yourself how you visualize your **seating plan** making sense. Talk to more experienced early childhood teachers who have done this before. Try what you think might work for you and your class. I have provided a suggested floor plan as an initial guide for you. I like this plan because the children are sitting in small groups. This helps them to get familiar with

Figure 4-7 Classroom Map

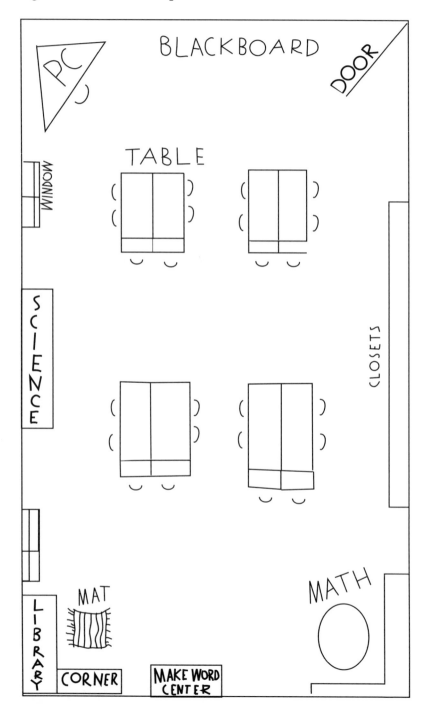

each other. It helps you to distribute papers and materials to a few tables instead of individual desks.

The only **drawback** to starting with **small groups** instead of rows is that all the children are not facing one way. If you think you've received a group of children who cannot handle sitting in groups because you won't be able to get their attention, don't hesitate to reorganize the individual desks so that all the children are facing you.

When you feel more comfortable, after your positive behavior plan is in place and you have gained the respect of your students, rearrange the desks into small groups. When you look at your room set-up and are ready to go, ask yourself these questions. Besides these student desks, are there places to write comfortably? Is the library set up? Is there a Science Center where you can set up interesting displays the children might enjoy discovering? Have you set up your math area complete with stored manipulatives, books and your calendar display? The more you anticipate the arrival of your students the smoother your first few days will run. This organization will give you a boost of confidence. It will look like you have set up a classroom before and chances are you might even start believing that you have (See Figure 4-7).

Staying Organized

You will need a **file** in which to keep important worksheets and school bulletins. Sure, it would be easier to use your creative idea once and then discard it, but remember it is worth saving your best ideas for future years. In time, you will collect various ideas for reviewing a number of subject areas. You can also share those that have worked for you with another new colleague. Two heads often work better than one and over time you will benefit when colleagues come up with a perfect activity or lesson for you. Of course, you might have a group of children next year whose abilities are very different from your first class. Don't chuck those files yet. They will come in handy one day.

Keep your desk neat, but don't worry if you cannot see the blotter sometimes when you are in the middle of helping your students finish a project. This mess doesn't mean you are not good at teaching. It does mean things can get messy when you work with children. If you had the perfectly neat classroom at every minute of the day, you probably would not be varying the activities in your classroom enough and you would be running the risk of boring your students to distraction. Keep everything in perspective. Do the best you can to keep your desk organized, but if it doesn't happen one

Supply List

☑ One large zippered transparent case
☑ One box of crayons (set of 16 or 24)
☑ One eraser
☑ Three sharpened pencils daily
☑ A pocket folder
☑ A ruler
☑ A bottle of white glue
☑ A covered pencil sharpener
☑ Two notebooks
☑ A roll of paper towels
☑ A box of tissues

Figure 4-8
Supply List

Check out whether or not the school is purchasing the supplies?

day, just regroup after school or before the children enter the classroom again in the morning.

As far as supplies go, you can begin with the basics. Have a can of sharpened pencils, a number of red and blue pens, some soft erasers for beginning writers, paper for the children to draw on, and lined paper for the children to write on. Have **supplies for the writing center** ready for use when that time comes. You will need red and black markers, and chalk and erasers right away. Purchase a set of sticky-backed name tags which your children can use the first day of school. Treat yourself to a good electric pencil sharpener which will be for your use only. They are worth their weight in gold.

Write a letter to the parents and guardians asking them to label their children's books and supplies with their names. Remind them to also label lunch bags, so as not to cause any problems (See Figure 4-9).

Find out what supplies will be purchased for the children by the school and what needs to be supplied by the parents. Make-up a short list of supplies the parents may need to purchase and attach it to the parent letter, if need be (See Figure 4-8).

Figure 4-9 Parent Letter
*Make this letter part
of the child's homework
to be returned to you.*

August 14, 2005

Dear Parents,

Welcome to the new school Year! I'm sure it will be a productive year filled with learning and excitement! I am looking forward to teaching your child.

From time to time I will be sending home information concerning our class program or upcoming events. Please make every effort to check your child's homework folder daily and respond if necessary. If you need to reach me for any other reason, please place a note in the homework folder and return it to me with your child in the morning. Of course, you can also reach the school office by calling this number ...
(or e-mail)

Attached you will find a list of supplies (see attached) that your child will need next Monday.

Thank you for your cooperation! I look forward to a productive year.

Sincerely,

Ms. Jones

PS: Please detach and return the form below with your child.

— — — — — — — — — — — — —

I have read the Parent letter and attached supply list

My Child's Name is ——————————————

Parent's Signature ——————————————

Date ——————————————

Collect all the glue bottles, store them in a shoebox on a shelf in your closet. Do the same with the rulers. These two items can lead to trouble if left too long in the children's desks. Use your imagination. When it comes time to use these items, initiate a lesson on how to use them appropriately.

The children will need to be shown how to keep themselves organized. Suggest ways in which they can organize the inside of their desks. Give them time to clean out there desks periodically. Discourage keeping any food inside the desks. Encourage them to keep notes that you are sending home in the pocket folder. **Role play** with them how they need to deliver the mail to their parent or guardian and return any replies the next day. Again, don't assume they will just do this without practice and reminders. Most of them probably won't. I can remember being shocked that no one in my class did a short homework assignment I had given them the first day of school. I said to a more seasoned teacher, "I can't believe it, no one did their homework." She wisely asked me, "Do you think they know what homework is?" **Don't assume** anything. By walking the children through the classroom set up and routines slowly and repeatedly you are insuring that they will be able to function easily and be able to set their minds on learning.

5

Readiness

The art of teaching is the art of assisting discovery

—Mark Van Doren

Have you ever had the opportunity to preview a movie before it was released to the general public? It can be an exciting experience. It's fun to know what happens at the end of the show before anyone else does. Doesn't it make you feel proud when you explain the plot to someone because you've had time to think about it and digest it?

Many **basic concepts** are introduced in the early childhood grades. Those children who are familiar with these concepts are excited! "I know that!" is a proud declaration heard. Those new to the basic concepts may feel frustrated early on. Besides formal lessons, it helps to offer children some short free form experiences through which they can start knowing what the teacher is talking about. They can begin to make connections and start saying, "I know that!" and they can begin to feel smart and proud of themselves. That is what you want, isn't it?

Positive experiences in school can breed more positive experiences. Its human nature. If you have good experience learning something you want to learn more because you were successful the first time.

While listening to a first grader read, I commented excitedly that he was doing very well. He had begun to read smoothly enough to read a whole sentence accurately. I paused a moment, looked in his eyes and asked him, "How did you do that?" He answered me honestly, "I don't know, my head did it."

Library Center Organization

This will be an important focal point of your classroom. Here your students will experience the world of Literature. Here you will share words, illustrations and ideas with your students. In turn they will share these books and ideas with their peers and discover what fun reading can be. They will begin the important process of incorporating **reading** into their lives, and hopefully, become lifelong readers and learners. You as a brand new teacher will have the exciting task of welcoming them to this world and showing them around. Your **enthusiasm** for teaching will be most needed in this part of your classroom. Some children might already be reading. Some will have been introduced to some authors before they enter the classroom. If there is an author who a few children are excited about, definitely explore his books with your class. You can start an author study on this author by adding reading activities that correlate with a few of each of her books. You can create these unit plans yourself or you can explore the ones that are available in teacher supply stores.

Organize your books in the library center according to categories or genres. For example, you can involve children in noticing that all true stories (nonfiction) are in one plastic basket and all storybooks about animals are in another. Go from there in deciding how you can group your books sensibly. Don't get too compulsive about this because children will not always return their books to the right baskets. Even doing this will be a learning experience over time. A short lesson about keeping the library orderly will be needed from time to time. You may want to create a basket which holds the books of an author the children enjoy. Tie attractive signs on the sides of the basket and store these on the shelves. Display a collection of fiction and nonfiction books on top of the shelves. Add a pretty plant or hang a mobile from the ceiling. Hang a sign announcing that this is the Library. Decorate in your own creative way. Have fun with it!

Children's Literature

There is an abundance of children's literature available to you. In the appendix of this book is a suggested **list of books** to help you begin your year. Consider this list an introductory one. As the stress of beginning the school year school year eases, explore the books of different authors.

Chapter Fourteen will help you do some guided reading with your children. This Chapter will help you go beyond the face value of a story and explore the children's understanding of a book. It also includes questions that will assist you in asking the children intelligent questions about their **reading** without having to prepare ahead of time. After going through these scripts one by one, you will start to understand the kinds of questions that are important for challenging your students' **thinking skills**. You will be able to apply this type of questioning to each academic subject, as well, to help your students delve into the why and how of the material they read.

Literature can serve as a wonderful introduction to a variety of subjects and as a springboard for many of your lessons. Begin an **index file** on those books that you find most helpful. After sharing a book with your class, write comments about the book and how it may serve you in future lessons. Maybe it's a story about a character that is looking for a friend and you might want to earmark this book for this time next year or for future lessons on cooperation. Those of you who prefer using a computer for your file can create a folder on Children's Literature that can be referred to at a later date. I have given this suggestion in literature courses I have taught at the College of New Rochelle and received positive feedback about it. It takes a little discipline to record the titles, authors and your reviews, but this information will come in quite handy next year. Again, you will be creating space to be more and more creative because you will have essential tools on hand.

Word Center Organization

Children will do what they do best here—explore. Start allowing small groups of students to visit the center about six to eight weeks after school begins. This will give you time to get to know your **students** and determine which students might **work well together**. In preparation, have a set of magnetic letters at the word center and a couple of magnetic boards. Also add a few small blackboards and some chalk. Place the "word wall" nearby. To introduce the children to this center do formal lessons with the whole class. Show your **excitement** for this opportunity to work independently on making words. Spend time discussing the best way to work with someone else at the center. Will they trace letters? Will they place letters next to each other to try and make a word? Will they show their partner a word they might know? Will they copy a word from the "Word Wall" that looks familiar? Talk about the importance of taking turns and showing manners when working with a partner. Teach the children how to take care of the materials at the center and how they must put all the materials away in their proper place when they are finished. Create a chart with the children by writing their words about these issues in simple sentences. After the chart is finished reread each sentence with the children and have then echo the sentences after you read them. You might also see if the children can remember certain key words in the chart by pointing to them in isolation. When this exercise is done, reread all the sentences in unison with the children. When you are ready to send a set of children to the center, review the chart with them. Don't expect that all will go well the first or second time. Remember that learning to work and working to learn together are both new experiences for the children. Try not to take it personally if things do not go well. You are learning too, but if you follow the advice I've just walked you through, you will be well on your way to a successful year as a brand new teacher.

Exploration is vital to reading readiness, and you must be willing to allow the children opportunities to use all their **senses** to learn. At the "Make Word" center they will see different types of letters, and they will be able to touch and feel letters. If you find that some children are not as familiar as others with their alphabet, you can provide them with letters cut from sandpaper which will help them learn the letters one at a time. Later on you can add a listening component to your word center by providing a tape recorder, head phones and tapes that review the letters and the nursery rhymes. *Little Miss Muffet* and *Humpty Dumpty* will remind your students of how reading works and coax them to notice how word families that rhyme can provide important clues to reading new words. You will have to do a group lesson to involve the students in using their sense of taste to experience letters. After reading the book *Stone Soup* by Jan Elliot, involve the children in making a cold soup using ingredients whose names begin with sounds you want to review: milk, cookie crumbs, sprinkles and bananas.

A Word Wall

"A Word Wall is a systematically organized collection of words displayed in large letters on a wall or other display place in the classroom." (Cunningham, 1995)

The Word Wall will become a point of reference in your classroom. Use a wide board to place the letters *Aa* to *Zz* evenly spaced across the top. It is beneath these letters that you must have enough space to add small word signs as you introduce these words in your lessons. To start, place the letters from left to right leaving room for lists underneath. From time to time add a word that you have introduced to your students through discussions or lessons. Add a few words that you've used to introduce certain initial **sounds**. At the start of the school year, spend about one week teaching and reviewing an initial sound. You will find a script for teaching a Phonics lesson in Chapter Eleven.

Your first **phonics** lessons will be to introduce the sound of the letter m. You will need to ask the children what words they know that begin with the sound of "m"; for example, the sound we hear when we say the word, man. When the children suggest other words that fit into this category, write them on a chart or blackboard and keep a record of these words. Choose which of these words you will use on the Word Wall. Make small signs of these words and add them to the board with the children the next day. Look for other opportunities to introduce **words**. With a rhyming lesson, for example, introduce a word by giving a clue such as, I'm thinking of a word that rhymes with cat and starts with "M" or "I'm thinking of a word that begins with the same sound as dog and ends with the same sound as fish."

As you move along in your program, you can introduce some sight words appropriate to a particular category. For example, during a lesson on the Season of Fall you may include the following words on your Word Wall: leaves, color, red, yellow, brown, trees. If you are presenting a lesson of friendship you may want to include these words: friend, share, help, and teach.

As you move through your day, if there is a word that you want to spotlight, show the children its location on the Word Wall and help them understand how the word is unique. What features does this word have that makes it like words the children may be familiar with? What other features does it have that make it unique and memorable? You want your students to get excited about learning and the best way to do this is to model enthusiasm for the way language works. It is this quality will make your classroom come alive. A teacher's **enthusiasm** is an essential key to motivating young children to learn!

You will find a basic list of sight words in the appendix of this book. This list, composed by **Dolch**, provides you with the **essential words** children need to learn. You will notice these words in many of the picture books and anthologies you use. This list is essential for choosing initial words for your Word Wall.

The Alphabet Chart

You have posted this chart before the children entered your classroom but you must remember that this chart is more than a decoration; it is a tool. You can use the alphabet chart to play many **learning games**. Such games can be used to introduce a formal lesson on a particular letter or sound or can be used in **transition** from one activity to another. The alphabet game is a great game to play at some time during each of the first days of school. While playing this game, you will be looking for children to help you find some letters on the chart. You will be singing a song to the tune of, *The Muffin Man*. Instead of the usual words you will be singing something like this, "Can you find the letter A, the letter A, the letter A, can you find the letter A, and show it to me?" Demonstrate how you will then choose someone whose hand is raised to come up and point to the letter A with the pointer. If he or she can find the letter, you will then lead the children in singing the second part of the song using the successful child's name: "Christine can find the letter A, the letter A, the letter A, Christine can find the letter A, she can show us." If the child happens to be unable to locate the letter A, calmly ask another volunteer to help her and then sing the second part of the song using both of their names. Always remember that play is one of the most familiar ways for children to learn. It makes the atmosphere non-threatening and helps you to succeed as a brand new teacher. If you are using this game as a transitional activity, continue with the game for no more than ten minutes and then proceed with the lesson at hand.

6

Setting the scene

They may forget what you said, but they will never forget how you made them feel

—Carl W. Buechner

When the curtain opens at the start of a play, your first impression of the scene helps to clarify the setting of the script. If your eyes focus on a city scene with bright neon lights you are reminded that the story takes place in a modern setting. What impression will the children get when they enter your classroom? Will it be a setting that excites their **senses** and beckons them to take part in learning? You are seeking a pleasant scene, attractive to the children, which introduces concepts in print and advertises them in an appealing way. This chapter will help you set up that backdrop even if you don't consider yourself to be artistic.

By now you have probably referred to the other chapters in Part Two. Desks and centers are physically in place; at least, in your mind. Now, you will want your room to reflect creativity, intelligence and educational knowledge. This chapter will introduce you to four elements of **design** that will help form this image. These four elements are contrast, proximity, alignment and repetition. These elements when combined can give a dimension of clarity to your displays.

Sometimes in our efforts to create a print-rich environment, we can make the mistake of displaying "too much stuff." When this happens, the imaginary frames around each piece are eliminated and it's difficult to focus on any particular image. The effect is chaotic and the ultimate effect on the students is confusion.

Work along with me in this chapter to create displays that are both clear and informative.

Planning is essential before touching any bulletin board, sketch it out on paper. Consider the lettering that has to fit in a specific space. Consider where you will display relevant projects. Study your classroom and plan for various displays. Try to align your Math Center near your Math bulletin board, and your Library Center near your Word Wall and Communication Arts bulletin board. Etc. Signage is important on all pieces children's work.

Design your world with color

Color is an important consideration. Different colors affect the mood of the classroom. For example, light blue is thought to have a calming affect on one's **mood**. On the other hand, it is a popular belief that children are stimulated by bright colors. Choose colors based on the effect you wish to create. (See Figure 6-10)

In preparation for the first day, choose a color for the background of your bulletin boards. This background paper will remain in use throughout the year. It will serve as a backdrop for all your displays of children's work. Add a **contrasting border** so that their work and artistic creations show up when you enter the classroom. You can identify contrasting colors that work well together by locating them on the color wheel (See Figure 6-10). Place your finger on the color red, for example. Now slide your finger directly across to the color green. These two colors are typically paired together but I suggest you consider using shades and tints of these colors. Electric green and bright pink are an eye catching combo. Another suggestion is to use a dark background with a brightly printed border. You can spend an afternoon at a teacher supply store considering what paper you will use for your brand new classroom. Have fun!

You can compare other color combinations in the same way:

| **peach & sky blue** | **orange & blue** | **yellow & purple** | **pale yellow & Lilac** |

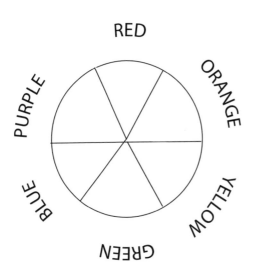

Figure 6-10
Color Wheel

A Board of a Different Color

Another appealing variation of colors you may wish to consider is the primary colors. These colors can be found by tracing a triangle on the color wheel.

The base of the triangle is formed by drawing a line from the color blue to the color yellow. From these two angles draw two angled lines that join at a meeting point forming the third angle of the equilateral triangle. If you circle the three colors you find at each of the three angles you've made, you have found the primary colors: red, yellow and blue. These three colors in combination are considered child-friendly. In combination, they are attractive and have been found to be stimulating to the **senses**. Open a catalogue offering the sale of accessories for children's rooms. Many times you will find this color combination.

To go one step further, consider how primary colors transform when they are mixed. If red and yellow are combined, orange is created. Now picture a yellow backdrop with a border in a red or orange print. Experiment with blue and red and their color combination purple or blue and yellow and their color combination green.

Bubble letters are commercially available and can be used to post general headings on bulletin boards. When you are finished using your first set of purchased letters this year, save them in a small box or sealed plastic bag. Next year you might want to recycle them by tracing them on colored paper in preparation for new titles on your boards. If you want your letters to appear three dimensional, try gluing a few small pieces of cotton behind them and then gluing them onto a piece of construction paper. Next, staple your sign on the bulletin board for an eye catching effect.

Contrast

Repeating color and contrast can bring pizzazz into your design. Teach the children a lesson on "Shadows," and make one of the lessons about Silhouettes. The Silhouette was an ingenious way to replcate an image of a person without drawing his face. It was created by Etienne De Silhouette who was the Finance Minister to Louis XV.

To create a Silhouette, you can sit each child sideways on a chair and hang a large black piece of construction paper behind her. You can use an overhead projector to shine a light onto her face. The resulting shadow will form on the black paper. Now take a piece of white chalk and draw the outline of the shadow you see. When this outline is cut out, mount it to a contrasting color. Neon colors work well; white is another option. I suggest you do this activity over a period of days unless you have another adult to help you. When all the projects are completed, you are ready to display them.

Some contrasting designs to use:

Math
Counting numbers

Size and color contrast ↑

Student Art Projects

← *Direction as contrast*

↑ **Silhouette**
color contrast

Proximity

Follow the old adage, "A place for everything and everything in its place." This pertains to print, supplies and work pieces that the children complete at the end of a lesson.

The room is ready for what I call "personality" and proximity can create this. Start with a bulletin board, for example, SCIENCE. Add a subheading that will introduce the objective of the lesson you have taught using contrast to show that this is a SCIENCE bulletin board. The subheading might be written in the form of a question, "How do plants grow?" Now you will want to keep the childrens three dimensional projects in close proximity to this board. They have grown some small plants from seeds. Place these on a table nearby and you have begun to create a SCIENCE center. You have a beautiful poster of fresh flowers—add a chart that diagrams the parts of the flower for future reference. Perhaps you have interviewed a parent volunteer about her garden and you have recorded it on an experience chart. By rounding up these pieces and placing them in close proximity, you are focusing the observer's attention, and this is essential.

The principle of proximity at work in this Science Center

Alignment

Imagine an imaginary line that runs from the top to the bottom of your board on the left side. Unless you are creating a collage effect, hang the childrens work along this imaginary line. Now, move left to right along an imaginary horizonatal line and add other pieces of work. From there you will want to begin another row with pieces directly below each thing you have hung horizontally.

Use a ruler to judge where the imaginary lines goes. Involve a colleague to get an extra set of eyes to help you. Alignment can be tricky and the lack of it can work against your design.

The alignment in this example is to the left. The alignment could have easily been to the right, top or bottom. Stick to whatever alignment you choose throughout your classroom.

Repetition

Using a repetitive theme will help to unify a classroom; it will make the classroom appear more cohesive. You can repeat color, or contrast or a border as a repetitive element to unify a room; you can use stars or bullets as a repeitive element, too. Try to use only one element for the best effect.

For example, you choose stars to frame all information concerning Communication Arts. Use same stars to frame information in the Math and the Reading areas of the classroom, too. Stick to that same repetitive element throughout the classroom.

If you are short on wall space and have to split up your math area, make a repetitve element for the sole use of Math. For example, use a border with an patriotic effect such as red, white and blue stripes around math information on one wall. Continue the effect on another wall, if that is where math is too. Subconsciously, it will be easier for a child to connect the dots, and know that red, white and blue stripes signify math.

↙	**Contrast**
↙	**Proximity**
↙	**Repitition**
←	**Alignment**

Using the rules of design as explained above will enable your bulletin boards to "pop" with personality. Use the rules of design first on paper and then add the children's work to the board. Step back and be amazed at the dramatic effect you have achieved!

Part **3**

Resources

Comprehension: Use the questions below as an aid to reinforce comprehension of the chapters.

General Art Projects

📖 What art project can be used in connection with a math lesson?

📖 What art project can be used in conjunction with a social studies lesson?

📖 What art project can the children bring home and use?

Interpreting Math Goals

📖 How can "playing games" be used to teach math?

📖 How are the senses, touch and hearing, related to learning math?

📖 What recurring classroom management activity can be used to learn counting?

📖 How can thinking about Shape, size and balance lead to endless activities to aid in teaching math?

📖 Explain how spatial learning is related to math.

Lesson Plan

📖 Can you ad-lib a lesson sometimes?

📖 How does motivation relate to the lesson plan?

📖 The lesson plan example in this chapter is about germs. Do you have any personal experiences with germs that you can relate to the children?

📖 Look at the Day One Scripts in Chapter Eleven. Create a lesson plan for Day One based on the what you learned from this chapter?

Props to enhance the Set

📖 Are some props more important than others? In this chapter, what is the most important prop?

📖 Assuming you have your subject areas set-up such as math and reading, where would you place the prop called reminder chart?

📖 How could you use design from chapter 6 to make a prop stand-out to the children?

📖 How would you use the props with the seating plan in chapter 4?

7

General art projects

"Every artist was first an amateur."

—Ralph Waldo Emerson

Teaching the early grades frequently requires you to act like a magician. You are expected to weave many subjects together so that your students are learning in a holistic way. When you teach a lesson in science, or social studies, you are incorporating skills from math and of course reading. You can choose children's literature from both nonfiction and fiction to support the unit that you plan to teach. If you are studying your neighborhood, you might consider using any of the following materials: pictures, a simple map, poetry, or an appropriate book. You might then guide the children to create photographs, drawings, graphs or arts and crafts projects which will celebrate the neighborhood. You can pull a unit of study together through skillful planning. If this sounds like a difficult or impossible trick to you, I am not surprised. Through experience, you will become more and more knowledgeable about the types of **activities** you can use to improvise for various lessons. This book will take you there right now.

I am going to give you some generic art activities that are simple and can be adapted as a follow up to many different lessons. You will use them

now and five years from now because they are basic. When introducing any project, hang up a model of the finished product beforehand. Encourage the children to be creative with their own finishing touches.

Aim: To Create a Paper Plate Note Holder

MATERIALS: One whole paper plate ✳ One half paper plate ✳ White glue ✳ Crayons

PROCEDURE: Show the children how to glue both pieces described together. Show them how they can use their crayons to make a pattern on the outside ridges of the plates. Decorate the plates with pictures that are appropriate to the theme you are discussing. Optional Step: Place a piece of colored tissue paper in the pocket of the project. Remember to have the children write their names on the back of the project. (See Figure 7-11)

CONCLUSION: After they are collected, punch a hole in the top-center of the project and thread a bright piece of yarn to provide a loop

Aim: To Create a Hat for All Seasons

MATERIALS: Use a length of sentence strip or other long narrow strip of heavy weighted paper ✳ Use an appropriate template ✳ Consider a star, a happy face, a frog, a snowflake, a shamrock, a flower or another four inch shape.

PROCEDURE: Distribute a length of sentence strip that will fit around a child's head. Instruct the children to decorate the sentence strip with colors or pictures that are appropriate for the lesson taught. Next have them decorate the shape you have chosen. Staple the colored shape to the center of the child's sentence strip. (See Figure 7-12)

CONCLUSION: Hold the sentence strip around each child's head, overlap the ends and then remove it from their heads and staple it to form a hat. Remember to keep the smooth side of the staple on the inside of the hat. This will prevent the children from being scratched by the staples edges

Aim: To Create a Box or Basket

Material: Use a piece of paper measuring approximately 9x12 or wider ✳ Crayons

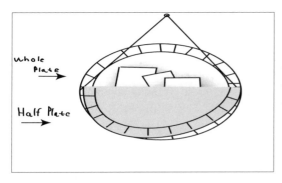

**Figure 7-11
Note Holder**

*Half paper plate
glued over full full
paper plate*

**Figure 7-12
Seasonal Hat**

**Figure 7-13
Boxes / Baskets**

*Draw the design
and folds on a piece
of paper first. See
example in lower
left corner.*

**Figure 7-14
Collage**

PROCEDURE: Provide a prepared paper for each child. Make the folds and draw the dotted line before distribution. Show them how to place their scissor on the edge of their paper and cut on the dotted line. Model how you do this being very dramatic about the need to stop cutting at the end of the dotted line. "Look, the road stops here, so we must be sure to stop." Allow the children to decorate according to theme. (See Figure 7-13, previous page)

Tell the children to hold the paper horizontally. You can help them visualize this concept by saying, "Hold your paper the hamburger way." Bring up the bottom third and fold it on the line and then open it. Have them do the same. Bring down the top third of the paper and fold it. Have them do the same. Next fold the three side pieces up on both sides. Have them do the same. When the side flaps marked with an X are folded over the center side flap you will have created an opened rectangular box. Staple the sides to secure it.

CONCLUSION: If you leave the open side of the box up you can create a basket from it by adding a handle, looped from side to side. If you choose to have them make a house, demonstrate how to draw bricks or stones before folding and stapling it together. Afterwards give them small pieces of colored paper to create doors, windows and chimneys. Of course the opening of the box will face down.

Aim: To Create a Collage

A collage can be made from a variety of small pieces of paper or material glued to a larger piece of paper. The small pieces do not have to be cut in an exact fashion. They can even be torn from magazine pictures or scraps of colored paper. They are glued all over the larger piece of paper helter-skelter according to the artist's eye. They can overlap at times.

In the early childhood grades the beauty of the finished piece is truly in the eye of the beholder. Because of this, the **children always succeed** and it is a great learning experience.

MATERIALS: Use large sheets of white paper ✳ white glue ✳ Paper for the collage (given scraps of paper the children can tear or cut their own pieces). (See Figure 7-14)

PROCEDURE: Talk to the children about a collage. Read a story which is illustrated with collage, for example, The Hungry Caterpillar by Eric Carle. Model for the children how they may choose to design their collage. "Do you want to group the same color pictures together? Do you want to have a variety of different pictures splashed all over?" Encourage them to do it the way they feel they want to by saying' "I can't wait to see what you are going to make!"

Aim: Spots before My Eyes

This project **works well with Math** helping the children make number sense. It can also be used simply for creative decorating.

MATERIALS: Provide each child with a light colored paper and about six circles

PROCEDURE: You can provide them with a large template of an animal which they can glue the spots on. They can also draw links between the dots to form a necklace. You can have them count the dots on the necklace and write the total number on their paper or note how two sets of different colored dots add up to a total number. Another alternative is to brainstorm ideas with the children about how they can add lines and drawings between the dots to form pictures. Model the different choices or just give them one particular set of directions and encourage them to be creative. (See Figure 7-15, next page)

Aim: To Create a Rainbow Plate

This project can be used as a **review of colors**. Other suggestions include a **lesson on friendship** and the beginning of a project that includes leprechauns and shamrocks.

MATERIALS: A set of gumdrop shaped paper that will fill the space of the top half of a paper plate ✳ A set of paper plates cut in half (each child will get one of these halves) ✳ A set of crayons with the basic colors ✳ White glue

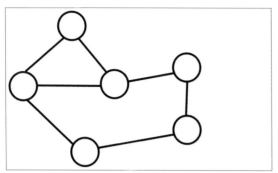

Figure 7-15
Spots

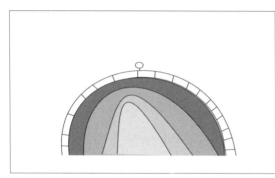

Figure 7-16
Rainbow Plate

Half-plate shown

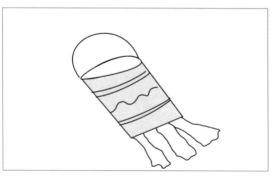

Figure 7-17
Windsock

Figure 7-18
Door Hanger

PROCEDURE: Guide the children to draw a small gumdrop at the center of the straight edge of the larger gumdrop paper. Instruct them to color their small gumdrop red. Next show them how to draw "over the rainbow" with the next color of the rainbow, orange.

Continue giving this last direction one at a time until all the colors of the rainbow have been completed: yellow, green, blue, and indigo and violet; I leave indigo out as it is not in the basic crayon box.

Next show the children how to take their completed rainbow and glue it to their paper plate piece. The curved side of the rainbow should be placed below the rounded edge of the piece and under the rim of the plate.

Encourage the children to explore all the colors by coloring each rim of the plate piece with the crayons of their choice. Suggest a pattern of colors or a random selection. Ask the children to write their names on the back of their work and collect them (See Figure 7-16, previous page).

Aim: To Create a Windsock

This is a project that is of many uses because it can be adapted to many holidays or themes. The main body of the windsock can even be formed from a picture the children have made (See Figure 7-17, prevous page).

MATERIALS: A paper approximately 12 by 14 inches ✀ A set of streamers or strips cut from colored tissue paper

PROCEDURE: Have the children hold their paper vertically. You can refer to this way of holding the paper as, "the hot dog way." After working on a specific theme, ask the children to decorate their paper appropriately-model some suggestions.

Next, collect these papers and form each into a cylinder. Overlap the edges and staple at the top and at the bottom. You can also punch hole in the sides of the top of each paper and tie on a bright colored yarn with yarn or ribbon to serve as a handle.

Aim: To Create a Door Hanger

MATERIALS: A door hanger shape ⚝ Crayons

This is a quick and easy project but one that the children enjoy **taking home and showing off**. Here again, pictures about any particular theme can be used to decorate it. (See Figure 7-18)

PROCEDURE: After a lesson, present each child with a door hanger that can be hung on a door at home. Show the children how the open hole fits around the door knob in the classroom.

Encourage the children to draw simple pictures about the topic at hand. Small pictures work best. Always provide some simple lessons on how to draw these pictures and encourage them to be creative.

CONCLUSION: Try a few of their door hangers on a door knob.

Aim: To Create Chunk Shapes

Collect templates for various themes and keep them handy in a large portfolio. They should be about 4 or 5 inches wide. You can collect them as you go along and always save sets of them for another time. The outlines of these templates should be as simple as possible so that after tracing them, the children can cut them out. Both of these skills are important to assist children in **enhancing** their **small motor coordination**.

MATERIALS: A set of templates for tracing, for example stars, fish, trucks, cars, flowers, and trees ⚝ Crayons

PROCEDURE: After a lesson on a given theme, distribute an appropriate set of templates. Show the children how to draw around the outside of the template and remove the template and notice the picture they find on their paper. Instruct them to color their work.

CONCLUSION: These pictures can be cut out and glued to another background paper or shape and displayed. See Figure 7-19, next page)

Figure 7-19
Chunk Shapes

A Personal Note

Some days, you'll know what you are teaching and how you are going to go about it but you're not quite sure what project you can do to wrap it all up. Refer to this chapter when you're stuck for a follow-up project. You may already know this feeling. You will be amazed at how many beautiful projects will come from the directions presented in this book. As you start to display some of this work, the more experienced teachers will be thinking that you really have it all together and you may even start to feel the same way.

" JASON, THE STICK FIGURES WE'RE DRAWING DO NOT
   HAVE TO BE ANATOMICALLY CORRECT. "

75c

8

Interpreting math goals

"And you will succeed? You will indeed! (98 and 3/4 percent guaranteed)"

—Dr. Seuss

A conductor of a symphony is asked to add a creative layer to a good story line. It is through his keen interpretive sense that a writer's intent is delivered to the audience. Math is a complex story line that starts out with a basic plot in the early grades. The key to being a successful conductor is to provide the children with the **multi-sensory activities** which will help them connect to and understand the basic concepts. By adapting the ideas presented in this chapter you will open up a multitude of learning opportunities for the children throughout the school year.

Even now, from the start, you can begin to be aware of providing a rich learning environment. You have put your Math materials in place around the classroom. These props can provide a visual reference point for the children. You will begin to take **attendance** from the first day and show the children how **counting** is applied to this daily task. You will begin to orientate the children on using small math manipulatives when working with a team member to create sets. You will be introducing picture books about

counting that are referenced in the Appendix of this book. You will use tapes and videos to reinforce math concepts in a fun way. Chanting counting rhymes and singing songs about numbers will provide a **transitional** activity and serve to reinforce important initial math concepts.

The Sense of Touch

Early in the year you can make **counting books** with the children. After a lesson which focuses on one particular number set ask the children to write the number on a paper and draw that many pictures to illustrate that number. Keep this work in simple individual file folders and when the worksheets on the numbers one to ten have been completed guide them to create a cover for their book You can prepare these covers by writing the word "Numbers" on it with a magic marker and allowing them to use crayons to write all the numbers they would like around this word. Finally, collect all the folders and attach the pages together to make a book. When assisting the children in forming their numbers, model the correct strokes and point out the number line as a point of reference.

Another time try the Spots art activity described in chapter 7. This is a fun activity because it allows the children to use their imaginations to form **designs** and pictures using dots. At the same time it allows them to touch the dots and count the dots they are using.

Learning through Play

When showing the children an example of sets and adding sets, let the children participate in forming sets themselves. Involve them in standing, holding hands and counting off. Use **games** as opportunities to reinforce **basic spatial concepts**. For example, when the children play the game, "Bluebird" the children are asked to form a circle. They are asked to hold hands and raise their arms to allow someone to pass under them. Now a leader is asked to weave in and out of these openings as the children sing. Notice that when the children are weaving in and out they are singing the word, "through" repeatedly and they are experiencing what this word means. This is much more powerful a learning experience than trying to explain what the concept *through* means.

When playing the game "Loopty Loo" the children repeatedly sing the words to the actions that they perform. The put their right hand in and out and repeat these directional words with their feet, elbows and heads. They are also experiencing following a sequence in this game.

The game "Duck, Duck, Goose" is a popular game which involves the children in forming a circle and sitting down. A leader is chosen who walks around the outside of the circle and taps the children on the shoulder as he chants, "Duck, duck, duck, and then he says the word goose when he decides to choose someone. That person then follows him around the circle and tries to tag him before he sits down at his original place. Notice that the children can pick their own sequence when choosing someone as the 'goose" Here a child has the opportunity to use **his own chosen pattern**. For example, he can say "Duck, duck, goose and repeat that sequence or he can say "Duck, duck, duck, goose." Etc. Whatever pattern he chooses, he is listening to his chant and every other child who takes a turn. He may subconsciously conclude how a pattern might work.

At some point in gym you may involve the children in a **relay race**. Here, different teams of four or five children line up and sit on one side of the gym. You will model for the children, how this particular race is played. For example you might ask the children to walk to a spot and grab a plastic ring and bring it back to the first child on his line. He must then sit at the end of his line. Now, the next child will have to take the ring back to the other side of the room then bring it back to the first child on his line. Notice the concepts involved are the formation of a line and following a repeated sequence of events, both of which are used in **Math reasoning**.

Using the sense of **touch** is invaluable to helping to ensure an under-standing of mathematical reasoning. You must be careful not to assume that because the initial concept seems like common sense to you, that the children will understand them as soon as you tell them about it. Yes, you may have those children who have picked up concepts at home or in earlier classes, but you will have those who have not. Remember, maybe some children were not ready to pick up those concepts earlier and they need you to teach them. Your richest teaching will come from involving educational activities which you allow as part of your lessons. When introducing any concepts about sets and comparing sets and changing sets through addition and subtraction, **allow time for the children to use counters**.

Playing with **blocks** is another opportunity for ah-ha moments. Here they are using different shapes and numbers of blocks to form new objects. Do they need the same number of blocks to form the same size columns? What blocks will help them form the house they are trying to make? Can they use two different blocks to place together which will mimic the size of another longer block? Now they might start to internalize that they can take a set of two and three and add them together to make five and they can use this newly formed block in the same way they use the five blocks. These conclusions are personal ones and you don't always know exactly what the children understand from play. Be assured that they are being exposed to opportunities that can only help them to learn and you will see the results in more traditional math activities

Move around the room during play time and mention that you notice what blocks they are using. Compliment them and always make your comment specific. Ask them questions about what they are making or what their plans are for their project. Give some suggestions. Mention words that will get them thinking. Interpret what they are doing and make suggestions that might work for them. **Think shape, size and balance**. Speak to them using words like **inside, outside, around and through**. As a conductor of this activity you will be a facilitator for learning. Your involvement is vital.

From time to time you can plan to prepare a special **recipe** with the children. This is a fun activity and involves many different math concepts. Pick a recipe that is easy, such as making an instant pudding. Talk to the children beforehand about the ingredients and materials you will need to gather in preparation for making the pudding. Discuss which parent volunteers might be able to help you with this recipe. Point out that you intend to make at least four batches of the recipe so that everyone can get involved. Each adult will assist a group in adding ingredients to make the pudding. Mention the tools that will be needed to measure the ingredients and blend the ingredients together. Use this opportunity to record all this information. Next list the steps that you plan to take to complete the recipe. The children get excited about this type of activity and appreciate that they will be rewarded for their efforts with some nice cold pudding. Remember to check beforehand to make sure that none of the children are allergic to any of the ingredients. (See Figure 8-20, next page).

Figure 8-20
A Recipe

We can make pudding!

Ingredients: four boxes of pudding
1 quart of milk

Supplies : four large bowls
four wooden spoons
one measuring cup

Directions: Pour one box of pudding
into one bowl. Add one cup of
milk. Stir Stir Stir.   Enjoy!

The Sense of Hearing

Allow each child to use his sense of hearing to solidify Math concepts.
Provide tapes and videos that review numbers in a fun way through chanting and song. There are also many **computer games** available to review
computation skills. Many of them ask the children to carry out a fun task
successfully if they can come up with the right answer. At some point the
children may understand the concept but need practice in coming up with
the right answer in a timely fashion. These games can sharpen this skill
and have a place in your math program.

Your Math symphony will be a dynamic one if you remember to utilize
the children's **senses** to bring them in tune with basic concepts. Follow
the scripts presented in this book to practice alternating activities as you
would musical instruments to reach with holistic harmony. You will feel
your confidence grow as you watch the children learn.

Personal Note

Teaching is a challenging career but one that will reward you for your efforts. In most cases you may not be rewarded with the amounts of money you see other people making but the rewards are those of satisfaction in helping children to become students.

During student teaching I was asked to do a science lesson for a first grade class. Having recently completed a course at St. John's University on science methods. I felt prepared and ready to go. My lesson would be nothing less than fabulous - I was going to create clouds. I was sure no else had bothered to do this in a first grade classroom and the children would love it. I came in with my equipment and proceeded to pump air into a heavy jug-type bottle filled with the required solution. Within minutes a cloud appeared. The children were mesmerized. One little boy looked at me with amazement and asked, "Can you make it rain tomorrow?"

Although the children could not actively participate in this activity because it was too sophisticated for their age level, their attention showed me that they were engaged in learning. This activity actually served as a **motivation for reading both fiction and non-fiction** books on evaporation, condensation and other related topics. It had served to engage the children as learners. I was engaged too as a brand new teacher and I felt great!

This book will clear the way for you to excite your children about learning. It will assist you in getting their attention and keeping it. It will teach you time proven teaching methods of teaching them. You'll be great!

Table 8-1 Measurements
Use these **measurements** for recipes with the children

	Equals (=)	Metric
1/8 Teaspoon		.5 ML
1/4 Teaspoon		1 ML
1/2 Teaspoon		2 ML
1 Teaspoon		5 ML
3 Teaspoons	1 Tablespoon	15 ML
1 tablespoon	2 Tablespoons	25 ML
4 Tablespoons	1/4 cup	50 ML
51/3 Tablespoons	1/3 cup	75 ML
8 Tablespoons	1/2 cup	125 ML
102/3 Tablespoons	2/3 cup	150 ML
12 Tablespoons	3/4 cup	175 ML
16 tablespoons	1 cup	250 ML
1 cup	8 fluid oz.	
1 cup	1/2 pint	
2 cups	1 pint	500 ML
3 cups		750 ML
4 cups	1 quart	1 LITRE
2 pints	1 quart	
4 quarts	1 gallon	

Lesson plan

"If you fail to plan, you plan to fail"

—Unknown

You may have received formats for lessons in your education courses but at this point they may represent only that to you, an outline. A lesson plan is, in many ways like a good movie. It gets your attention with an interesting plot. The script carries you through the story step by step. The quality of the script determines if the audience can see part of themselves in certain characters or situations. A viewer might make the statement, "I really related to that movie!" The movie ends when all the loose ends have been tied up. To initiate a successful lesson, you need to have an understanding of the concept of a lesson plan.

The lesson plan seeks to move you through a series of scenes in order to get across one particular **concept**. "One" is the key word here. It is important you **don't ad lib** so much that you find yourself off track completely. If the discussion or activity brings up other interesting discussions, acknowledge these ideas but note them for another discussion for another time.

Topic vs. Objective

It is important to distinguish between the topic of the lesson and its objective. The topic of the lesson would be considered general and the objective would explain exactly what part of the topic would be addressed in one particular lesson. Let's suppose you planned to teach a lesson on the topic of "Maps." If I decided to teach a similar lesson in the classroom next door, there would be little probability that we would be teaching a similar concept. You might decide to focus on the skill of finding directions on a map. You would pose questions like, "What could be found in the North section of the map or the South, East or West?" Without any discussion with you, I might also decide to teach a lesson on maps but decide to focus on making a simple map of the classroom. There is a clear distinction between the topic of maps and the particular objective that will be addressed in any one lesson.

Other objectives for a unit on maps may include any of the following:

- What is a map?
- What are the different types of maps?
- How can we use the key of a map?
- How can we plan to make a map of the streets around our school?
- How can we create a map of the streets around our school?

Consider Your Student

In order to understand the needs of your students, you need to understand their growth thus far. Understanding their prior knowledge of a subject prevents you from planning with a blindfold on. You do not want to introduce a lesson that is "above their heads." At the same time, if most of the children have had some experience with the subject, you don't want to bore them. You may want to review basic concepts during an initial lesson and offer creative activities at a work station for those who need more experience in basic skills. You may plan more challenging activities for those who are familiar with the subject. This creative approach will keep everyone engaged in learning.

Learning Style

Much has been written about the importance of awareness of learning styles. You will find that many children learn about maps through the use of them rather than through a lecture on them. As they actually trace a route on a simple map, they can begin to understand how a map can be useful. These children take a kinesthetic approach to learning. Their sense of touch helps make the concept real. Another child might come to an understanding when he listens to a book on tape about the concept of maps. In this case, he is utilizing his auditory and visual senses to help him take in the concepts presented. Seeing the map displayed in the classroom and discussed from time to time can serve as a constant visual reference. How might you utilize the children's sense of taste in this lesson? Plan a trip to the local ice cream store and mark it on the classroom map. Some children will remember this route!

Motivation and Procedure

A creative presentation can motivate children to learn by finding part of the topic that may be familiar to them. This is the motivation that drives the lesson. Read a picture book that touches on the topic of the lesson. Use a puppet to grab the student's attention. Use a game that goes with the topic at hand. Once you have the students' attention, you're halfway there. The discussions and activities that follow will flow naturally.

The procedure of the lesson lists the steps of an activity that will involve the children in the lesson allowing them space to internalize what has been hinted at so far. This hint has been presented through a motivational tool. Think of how a stand-up comedian grabs the attention of his audience. It is the element of surprise that does the trick. The element is as simple as a question or as interesting as a short media presentation.

Consider using simple objects you find around your house that call attention to the topic at hand. Show-and-tell does wonders to open up a dialogue. In the case of the lesson on maps, why not bring the topic into reality? Members of the community can be a valuable resource. Visit a local travel agency and explain that you are an early grade teacher who plans to teach a lesson on maps. They may provide you with a local map or the map of a family amusement park. Use these for future discussions about planning to visit that spot.

Props All Around

Think of what hobbies you are involved in; your skills may be creatively adapted for the classroom. I used my knowledge of photography to involve my students in creating a photo essay on "Friendship." We read books that contained the theme of friendship. We wrote about friendship. Next, I involved the parents in helping to obtain slide film. The children took slides depicting people demonstrating acts of friendship and from them we produced a slide set to music. The result was quite dramatic. Today, you can adapt this idea to digital software and consider using the computer to produce this type of photographic essay.

Procedure

Think ahead to create a logical set of steps the lesson will take Move from the broad idea of the concept you are presenting to the specifics of the objective you will be teaching. Model the skill when possible and allow the children to become involved in an activity after all parts of the concept have been discussed and reviewed.

The follow-up activity should be one during which the students can demonstrate their understanding of the concept that was taught. The timing of each part of the lesson should not be lengthy; the lesson should move along smoothly. Pacing is important becasue children have short attention spans. Any follow-up homework that directly reviews the concepts taught can be explained at this time.

If you are assigning a workbook page, assist them in circling the page number they will be working on. If you are distributing a worksheet, make sure they place this sheet in their work folder. Remind them that you will be checking this homework tomorrow.

Conclusion

This part of the lesson serves to review the concept that was introduced at the start of the lesson. This part of the lesson need not be formal or written. Simple questions will encourage students to reprocess the information that they have learned. A conclusion serves to bring a sense of closure to a lesson. Afew may listen to this discussion and just begin to understand the concept that was spoken about. A conlcusion also allows you to consider what knowledge the children may or may not have gained from this lesson. Armed with this understanding of your students, you are in a better position to plan future lessons on this topic or other lessons that will explore other specific objectives about the general topic being introduced.

The Lesson

This lesson was created in response to a health issue in the classroom. Children were coughing or sneezing and forgetting to cover their mouths and noses. In an effort to keep the children healthy, this lesson was presented. Some lessons will follow planned unit of study and others will spring from a specific issue. Practice being aware of the specific needs of your classroom community.

To Review How We Can Prevent Germs from Spreading

For a Health lesson concerning, "Keeping Germs Away" your **aim** might be stated, "To List the Ways We Can Stop Spreading Germs." You might introduce this topic by talking about an **experience** you had when someone failed to cover his nose and mouth when sneezing. Be dramatic! Children love when you let them into your world. Now allow them to share their experiences too. Lead them to some conclusions by **asking a question** like, "So how do you think we can prevent germs from spreading around the classroom? Write their ideas on a chart paper or blackboard. Always review these few simple statements by reading them together with the class. Next, you can introduce an art lesson which will help them to further relate to the concept.

Provide them with a copy of a simple drawing of a head (See Figure 9-21). Tell them that they can draw the eyes, nose and mouth to look like their own features. If possible, let them look in a mirror before beginning to color. It would help to have prepared a few samples of these head shots and hang them up as a model. Lastly, demonstrate how they can glue a tissue over the nose and mouth of their head shot and then overlap a ready-made hand, which you provide.

At the conclusion of the activity, tie up loose ends by asking them to share their work by holding their paper under their chins and taking turns saying something they may have learned about the prevention of germs. As the children give their suggestions, validate them with statements like, "Wow, that's great" and "Good for you!" You, as a director need to point out the positive about your cast members at every chance you get. They need to hear your words.

Figure 9-21
Lesson Plan

Table 9-2
A Sample Lesson Plan

Aim:	To List the ways we can stop spreading germs
Motivation:	Discussion of the topic
Art Activity Materials:	* Outline of hand and head * Cutout * Crayons * Glue * Tissue
Procedure:	* Discussion about the importance of covering hand and mouth when sneezing * Children will draw and color their own head and hand outlines * Children will glue on a tissue to the drawing and head and glue a ready-made hand on top
Conclusion:	Let the children share their art work and review concepts of spreading for understanding
Follow-up:	Ask children to bring their work home and share what they learned with a friend or family member
Note:	Remember to have them write their first names on their work or write it for them if need be.

A Personal Note

You are your own best fan and you can be your worst critic. Think of your first lessons as your first auditions and then first rehearsals. Try not to be perfectionist: teaching is really an art. There is nothing more satisfying as a lesson that went well. Maybe actors feel like this when they are appreciated and understood by their audience. It doesn't happen every time. With practice and perseverance it will happen more often. Teaching is a challenging profession. Teaching young children is a dynamic all its own. As you meet this challenge, you will be rewarded with tremendous satisfaction!

10

Props to enhance the set

"What its children become, that will the community become"

—Josh Billings

Theatrical props are vital to enhance a set. They paint a picture of where the story takes place. Theatrical directors ask their crew to collect props, so a scene is made believable to the period it takes place in. A classroom is no exception. Children must know they are in a learning environment! Without props the children get distracted. Children have short attention spans and props serve as a way to introduce and review **concepts**. If a child needs a reminder of a basic letter, word or number, props serve as a friendly security blanket. Words and sentences around the room will help children associate written and spoken words.

Words at work

"Words at Work" include titles on bulletin boards, name cards, rounds, reminder plaques, ID labels, a calendar display, a birthday display, a shape chart, a seasonal clock and an alphabet chart. These **props are the initial displays** that you will put into place **before the children enter the room** on the first school day. You'll be amazed at the transformation of your

brand new classroom. You will feel proud of yourself and you will be rewarded by the appreciation of your new students. Let's look at some props.

Name Cards

In Chapter Three I discussed the value of using name plaques. The short activity of calling out the names and distributing the name tags will be one more way you can begin to associate each child with his or her name. Leave the name plaques on the desk for the first several weeks. These plaques will provide the children with a model of their names to trace or copy. They can also be used as a **motivation** to teach the children the importance of knowing their full names, addresses and phone numbers. At the beginning go slowly and simply focus the children on the formation of the letters of their names.

Rounds

Make a set of circles about six inches in diameter. Prepare one for each child by writing the child's name in the same way you wrote the names on the name cards. These will be used to play the name game which is described in Day One's script. If you want to narrow down each child's choices, you can prepare the girl's names on one colored circle and the boy's names on another (See Figure 10-22).

Reminder Charts

Use small signs made from construction paper to serve as reminders for you and your students. You may have a few children who attend a **special program** like speech on a certain day. Note the day and the program on a sign and list the children who attend this program. Add the time of the program if you like. Display these small charts in a prominent place to remind you of what is happening each day. Provide space near these plaques to post school notices of **upcoming events** or administrative paper work that must be completed by a certain date. This practice will keep you organized and help you concentrate on the most important task at hand, teaching the children. (See Figure 10-23).

ID labels

Label obvious things around the room. You may need to refer to these labels from time to time to help the children make the sight and the sound connection between the written word and the spoken word. Label the window with the word window, the door with the word door. Label your desk, the class library, the closet, a book shelf, a plant and any other obvious

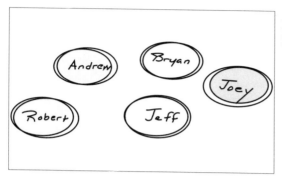

Figure 10-22
Rounds

Figure 10-23
Reminder
Charts

object in the room. Print each sign with a dark marker. You can use all lowercase letters for these signs.

Shapes

Create a chart of basic shapes and identify them by name. You can be creative by personifying these shapes, "Ms. Triangle" or "Mr. Square". Make your chart attractive by using the color combinations described in chapter three. This chart will serve as a reference for future **Math lessons**. The children will learn how to draw these shapes, how to recognize and identify them and how to use these shapes to complete given patterns. At the beginning, focus your lesson on the name and formation of one shape. Before a lesson allow the children some play time to work with small shapes. They can trace these shapes and create collages from them. Touching these shapes and exploring them will help the children internalize the concept of shape and help them get ready to identify the shapes they see in the objects around them (See Figure 10-25).

Calendar Display

Hang up a large calendar for September. Sometimes a wooden calendar may be provided for you. You might choose to use a large poster type

Today is Monday

It is September 30
It is a Fall Day
The Leaves are Falling

*We will read
about the leaves*

**Figure 10-24
A Calendar
Story**

**Figure 10-25
Shapes**

calendar which can be purchased in a teacher's store. Purchase a large blank classroom calendar and add only the dates of September up to the first day of school. Do not add the first date of school until you are working with the children on that day. The changing of the calendar and the discussions about the calendar will progress as the weeks of school go on. Focus on the number that signifies the date and the day of the week. Point out the name of the month and the season and open up a discussion about the signs you will all be looking for in nature that will mark the changes in the seasons. Choose **children's literature** which will help the children to understand the significance of the changing of the date, the month and ultimately the season (See Figure 10-24).

Birthday Display

A display of the children's birthdays helps to further develop their **sense of the timing** of the school year. Besides this, it also helps each child to appreciate his individuality. As children begin to pay attention to the information provided on the birthday chart, they begin to recognize each other and this recognition builds a sense of community in the classroom. These are all good things. Of course these charts are available commercially, but there is something nice about a homemade touch. Divide a poster board into twelve boxes and write the name of a month in each box. Use each box to print the names of the children who have a birthday that month. Also record the date of that birthday next to the child's name. Top off the chart by placing a picture of a birthday cake complete with a sign entitled, "Happy Birthday" This chart will be one of the most popular charts in the room. You will regularly find a few children walking over to it to check whose birthday is coming up and pointing out when they will have a birthday. After all, who doesn't want to be the birthday girl or boy?

Alphabet Chart

The classroom should have an alphabet chart on display all year. The letters can be purchased commercially. Choose a set that does not have a busy pattern. When children enter your class they might not already know their alphabet. Many times they need to review names and sounds at the beginning of the school year. They need to be exposed to activities that can reinforce the letter names and sounds. A **fun game** to play with the children is described in Day One's script.

A Seasonal Clock

This seasonal clock can be referred to **all year long**. Referring to it during discussions about the calendar will help the children understand the concept of the changing seasons. If you are in a climate that does not experience four seasons, adapt your seasonal calendar accordingly. Later on the children can make something similar with a paper plate and fastener. The paper plate can be divided into four quadrants by drawing a line down the center of the plate and a line across the middle of the plate from left to right. A fastener is used to attach a ready-made arrow to the center of the plate. The children should be given prepared plates and guided to draw pictures that represent the seasons. These seasonal clocks can be used to review the changing seasons of the year. Later on topics like the **thermometer and the temperature** will be built on these concepts that were introduced at the beginning of the school year (See Figure 10-26).

**Figure 10-26
Seasonal
Chart**

$\mathcal{P}art$ 4

Scripts

Comprehension: Use the questions below as an aid to reinforce comprehension of the chapters.

Scripts for a Week

Can you alter the scripts based on the ability of the children?
Note the transitional activities in the scripts. Can you think of any other uses for them?
What acting exercise below would be best for the lunch or the recess script?
(a) Voice (b) Pantomine
(c) Facial Fun

Creating Scripts

You have finished using the Scripts for a Week. What scrips would you create for Day 6?

Conflicts on the Set

🖹 What is Weeping Will really saying?
🖹 The most common behavior challenges are listed in this chapter. Can you think of any others?
🖹 From the examples given, could you create your own scripts for new behavior challenges?
🖹 If the behavior continues. What should you do?

Scripted Questioning Techniques

🖹 How would you use Bloom's Taxonomy with a story of your choosing?
🖹 What guided math activity would you use, if it followed the reading of, *Now One Foot, Then the Other*?
🖹 With this guided math activity, which one of the following thinking skills would you be using?
(a) Knowledge (b) Comprehension
(c) Analysis (d) Synthesis
🖹 What is the most frequent thinking skill question in this chapter?
(a) Knowledge (b) Comprehension
(c) Analysis (d) Synthesis

11

Scripts for a week

*"Life is like playing a violin solo in public and
learning the instrument as one goes on ..."*

—Samuel Butler

In this section of Brand New Teacher exact lines are presented for those first days of school. There will be no guesswork needed. It is all here. Each day offers a series of lessons, lines and activities which are appropriate for your early childhood class. These lessons can be used in September or at another time when you are first beginning a teaching term. The lessons are essential ones because they introduce initial orientation and provide you with valuable information about the skills your new students may or may not possess.

Pay careful attention to their abilities and take notes if necessary. Many times it is during lessons such as these that a teacher notices that a child may need remedial help early on. These lessons contain scripted lines that you may need only because you are a little unsure of how it will all come together. Add or subtract lines and lessons as you see fit. The scripts are not strictly timed. You will have to consider your schedule and decide how much time you have to devote to any of the activities. Don't dismiss this book after you have finished with the scripts. Instead, use it as a guide for writing future lessons and daily plans. This is where your creativity will come into play. Start slowly by fitting lessons into the type of routine you see described here. You will have to alternate quiet activities, fun activities and conventional lessons. Remember teaching young children is a little like presenting a magic show. You must keep their attention.

DAY ONE

Orientation
20 Minutes

You will have the children's name plaques on their desks when they enter the classroom (See Chapter 3 for information about name plaques). As they come in, guide them to stand on the sides of the classroom in a single line. Greet the children with a pleasant "Good morning!" and announce that you will now assign them their very own seat. One by one call out a name and bring that child over to his seat.

After the children have been seated, welcome them to their new class. Introduce yourself and print your name on the blackboard. Tell them how excited you are about this first day of school. Ask them how they are feeling but don't be surprised if they remain pretty quiet. It's been an exciting morning for them already. Tell them that it will be a wonderful school year and you are happy to be their teacher.

Announce that you will now take the attendance. Explain that this will be a daily routine, which means that every morning you will be saying "Good morning" to each of them and they will have the opportunity to say "Good morning" to you. Now is a good time to remind them of exactly what your name is and how it is pronounced.

Tell the children that when they hear their name and respond they are also invited to come up to you and share with you anything they'd like. Sometimes a child is excited about a family event, like a sister's birthday and would like to share that with you. Other times a child has a concern, such as he or she doesn't know who will be picking them up. He or she may have a note with them that their parent asked them to give you. Allowing a space in time for them to come up and share information can relieve them of anxiety before any lessons begin. I have found this simple morning routine to be invaluable. It builds a strong student-teacher relationship. It also keeps you organized and aware of each child as an individual. Sit on a chair during this activity but not behind a desk.

Reading Time

10 MINUTES

After this attendance routine is completed stand and face the children. Tell the children that you are excited about reading with them this year. Acknowledge that some of them will be learning to read for the first time and others may be able to read already. Ask the children questions that will open up the discussion about any prior experience that they may have with reading.

PRIOR KNOWLEDGE

▸ How many of you would like to read?
▸ Who knows how to read?
▸ Who is excited about learning to read this year?

In getting answers to these three simple questions you will begin to formulate what the needs of your students will be this year.

Next, write a simple sentence on the blackboard like, "The boy likes to play ball."

Ask for volunteers to read this sentence. You may find a child who volunteers but cannot read it at all. Comment, "Good try." You may find a child who can read one or two of the words. You may find a child who can read the sentence easily. Show excitement toward those that succeed and always encourage those who try but fail. If no one can read the sentence say, That was a good try! These words say, "The boy likes to play ball."

If you find any successful readers for the first simple sentence, try a more difficult sentence, "The sky lit up when the lightning began." This type of a sentence is a definite stretch for young readers, but it will help you find out if you have any children who can already read well.

Rhyme Time

30 MINUTES

Tell the children that you would like to tell them a story that you call, "The Rhyming Story." Your aim is to have the children hear the rhyming of one family of words. Later you can adapt this lesson for other word families, such as the short vowel sounds listed below (See Table 11-3):

Table 11-3

cat	sam	tag	had
rat	bam	bag	had
sat	jam	rag	sad
bit	big	hog	hot
sit	wig	fog	pot
mit	dig	jog	dot
cut	pug	pet	pen
hut	mug	met	hen
put	bug	set	men

sit bit

sit

sit mit

mit bit

mit

A Short Vowel Story

Once there was a little girl named *Nan*.
Spell Nan as you write the letters on the board.
She had a brother named *Dan*.
Spell Dan as you write the letters directly under the word Nan. Continue spelling and writing the family words as you elicit them from the children.

Use this story as a review of the AN Family

Their father was a very tall *Man*.

One summer day the temperature was 100 degrees. It was very hot so their father turned on the *Fan*.

Were hungry said *Dan*, so dad took out the *Pan* to cook some hamburgers.

After lunch, dad announced that they were all going to take a ride to the beach so the children *Ran* to get dressed.

Always make a concluding statement at the end each lesson by saying, "You have done a wonderful job, boys and girls. Wasn't that fun?"

At the beach, they had fun playing on the sand and in the water. They got a *Tan* from being at the beach.

What a great time we had today, said *Nan* as they got into their car to go home.

Wow, what a great story! It was about *Nan*

Review Words in the *AN* family

Point to the word and spell the letters.
And *Nan* had the brother named *Dan*.
Point to the word and spell the letters.
Dan turned on the *Fan*.
Point to the word and spell the letters.
Dad cooked lunch in the *Pan*.
Point to the word and spell the letters.
Remember how they *Ran* to get ready for the beach?
Point to the word and spell the letters.
And they got a *Tan*.
Now say, Lets review our rhyming words by spelling and saying each rhyming words on the list:

Nan   Man   Pan
Dan   Fan   Tan

Recess
10 Minutes

Consider allowing the children some time to relax and /or use the bathroom. Ask experienced teachers beforehand about what bathroom the children will be using or any details about a routine for recess.

Before any activity like recess, talk to the children about appropriate behavior. You must be careful to send only a few at a time into a bathroom and actually walk the class to the bathroom if it is not near the classroom. In any case, mention that it is important that they wash their hands before they return to their seats. Hand washing is the most effective form of germ control.

Math
10 Minutes
Counting

After recess settle the children into their seats and get their attention by saying, "Now that we are back, it is a good time to count how many children are in our class." Choose a girl to walk around the classroom lightly tapping each girl on the shoulder.

As she does this you can help her count the children. When she is done remind her to count herself too. Write this number on an erasable chart next to the word "Girls."

Repeat this procedure with the boys being sure to enter the total number of boys underneath the number of girls. Write the word "total" underneath the words "girls" and "boys" and explain this word by asking, "How many children do you think we have all together?" Count all of the children as one set and write the total number on the board.

Guided Math
20 Minutes

Now is a good time to have the children participate in a culminating activity on counting. Before you begin, guide the children to notice where we see numbers everyday. Talk about the clock, the supermarket, the bank and school. Show your excitement about their knowledge of numbers. Explain that now we will have a chance to do some work with these numbers.

Distribute a paper folded in or divided into eight boxes. You should prepare these papers before class. Tape one of these papers on the board. Distribute the papers to the children. Ask them to write their names on the back of their papers. Point to the upper left box and model how they can write the number one. Next to the number one suggest that they draw one ball. Note that the drawing is simple and expert drawing is not necessary. Continue asking them to recall a number, write the number and draw the necessary number of things to complete each set. Model as you go along. At the conclusion of this activity tell the children that they have done a wonderful job. This is not a time to draw attention to children who do not understand numbers. Encourage them to do the best they can and make a note of any problems for future planning.

A Finger Play

10 MINUTES

Transitional Activity

This finger play will provide a smooth transition into the next activity. Ask the children to stand after the Math work has been collected. Have them stretch with you by following your directions. Tell them that now we will be moving to the Library Area. Walk to the area and stand there. Call children a few at a time to come over to the area where you are standing. When all the children are with you at this area raise up both of your hands. Ask them to lift up both of their hands, too.

Announce that you are going to recite a "finger play" with them that they may or may not know. Recite this popular finger play using your hands to demonstrate the words:

Repeat it slowly, repeat it quickly.

Always have them use their fingers to animate the words

Open shut them, open shut them

Give a little clap

Open shut them, open shut them

Put them in your lap

Creep them, creep them, gently creep them

Rght up to your chin

Open wide your little mouth

But do not let them in

A Read Aloud

20 MINUTES

Plan the story you will read. A few examples for appropriate stories are included in the appendix of this book.

Discuss the title of the book and the author and illustrator. Discuss the cover by asking them if they can guess what this book might be about. Using the terms author, illustrator, cover, pages, beginning, middle and end will help the children become familiar with them as the school year progresses. Open the discussion to see if the children have any prior knowledge about the theme of the book. Read the story slowly and show the pages as you go along. I suggest that you discourage discussion during the reading of the book and gently suggest talking about it when the story is finished and everyone has found out what happens. After the book has been enjoyed and the discussion is complete, end the session and send the children back to their seats.

10 MINUTES

If you have a small block of time, you may want to give them the opportunity to draw a picture in response to the story. Some may draw a picture. Some may write a word or two. Any response is great! Say so.

Orientation walk

15 MINUTES

If you have any other time available, I would suggest that you take the children down the hall to help familiarize them with at least part of the school. If you are working in a large school, you may have to coordinate the timing of this walk with your supervisor.

Lunch Prep

15 MINUTES

At least twenty minutes before lunch, discuss any necessary routines. Reassure the children by telling them who will be in charge of this activity if you will not be there. Tell them that you will be picking them up after lunchtime and show them where you will be picking them up. This may seem like common sense to you but remember it may be new for some of them and they will need your support.

Tip Toe Train
10 Minutes
Transitional Activity

After lunch, settle the children in their seats and help them put all their lunch boxes and jackets away before you get back to work. The following game will help them relax after an exciting lunch period.

Explain that you will choose one child to be the train's engineer. This child will silently tiptoe around the classroom looking for someone who is not peeking to become the next engineer. Instruct the children at their seats to put their heads on their desks and close their eyes. As each new child is picked, he becomes the lead engineer. The line becomes longer and longer with each new engineer added to the front of the line. The only child who ever picks another child for the train is the current engineer. Tell the children that it is important that no one speaks during the game and that the children on the line remember to tiptoe. The game ends early if someone speaks. At the end of the game, guide the children to count off to reach the total number of children on the train. Not only is this game fun, it gives the children an experience with cardinal numbers. (You may also change your counting style by using the ordinal numbers, "First, second, third ..."

The Name Game
10 Minutes

Remember those rounds (see chapter 10) you prepared with the children's first names written on them? Now you are going to use them to play a game. Tape all the names to a wide board. Tape them at eye level for the children. One by one ask the children to tell everyone their name and then go up to the board and find their name in print. When they successfully find their name, compliment them. If someone cannot find his name, assist him inconspicuously.

Homework
10 Minutes

Did you know that children sometimes do not know what the word homework means? Don't assume that they do. Discuss the fact that the word homework is made up of two words, "home" and "work," and so the word refers to the work we do at home. Talk about the responsibility involved in homework.

Tell the children that they will have one job for homework tonight. Their job will be to take home the parent letter which talks about the supplies they will need for school. (You may have been given other forms from the office that you will have to include with this letter). Tell them that you will be collecting any papers that are returned by their parents in the morning. Tell them that you will be reminding them in the morning to take out any letters from their parents, so that they can bring them to you when their name is called.

Dismissal
20 Minutes

Give yourself at least thirty minutes to prepare for dismissal. You need to allow this time so that the children are not rushed. Call a few children at a time to gather their things from the closet or nearby shelf. Next, have them pack what they will be taking home and listen to what the routine of dismissal will be. Know what this procedure is yourself. Bring your class list on a clipboard so that you can jot down any information from a parent or guardian. Assure the children before leaving the classroom with them that you are not in a hurry and are looking forward to meeting all their parents, relatives and baby-sitters.

As the last child is picked up, congratulate yourself on a job well done! The day might have had a few challenges that didn't follow the script but imagine what would have ensued without one!

DAY TWO

Orientation
20 MINUTES

As the children enter the classroom, give them an opportunity to find their seats. Remember, move slowly, a few at a time. Remind the children how they will walk to the closet and put away their jackets and empty book bags. Also remind them where they should put their lunch boxes. Finally, remind them to take out any notes they may have brought you and put them in the upper corner of their desks. As the children settle into their seats, get their attention with a kind yet firm voice and begin taking attendance. As you get notes and forms from the children, place them into specific piles and clip them together so that you can tend to them at a later time.

Morning Message
15 Minutes
Reading

Gather the children at a meeting center in the Library Area (page 52). Have chart paper or an easel or board near you. Begin the discussion and lead the topic to the day, date and weather. You can ask the children what day it is and then write a child's answer as you repeat their words one at a time. Your chart may look something like this when the discussion is finished:

Today is Tuesday.
Today is September 9, 2004.
It is a sunny day.

Have the children echo the reading of this chart. You may now want to show a few features about some words that make them unique. For example, you may point out that the word "today" is a compound word made of two words: to and day. Have the children hold their chin and slowly say the word. Ask them how many times their chin went down when they said the word today. The correct answer is "two" because the word "today" has two syllables.

Certain words like Tuesday and September should be treated as sight words; they should not be sounded out but only remembered through repeated exposure.

Word Game
10 MINUTES

Tell the children that you will now play a listening game. Explain to them that you will be saying a set of two words. Tell them that they need to be very quiet and listen to see if the two words they hear rhyme. If they do rhyme they can signal yes by touching their ears. Here we go...

night & **light**

see & **me**

tint & **mint**

big & **bell**   ☒

send & **bend**

fill & **fell**

This game does not require you to write the words on a chart but you may want them available on a chart to use for another day during a phonics lesson.

Guided Reading
20 Minutes

Prepare a chart ahead of time with the words to "This Old Man," an English folktale. This will be the first poem you introduce to the children. After reading it and revisiting it a few times, you can laminate it and hang it somewhere near a meeting area in your room. Eventually, you'll have a selection of poems that you can focus on for guided reading.

Enjoy the poem with the children and have them reread it with you. Ask them which words rhyme when you read lines one and two. Do the same with lines three and four. Ask them what words rhyme with the word "three" and what words rhyme with the word "four." Read it again, sing it again. Go back and point to each word as you read it together slowly...

This Old Man

English Fold Song

This old man, he played one,
He played nick-nack on my drum
With a nick-nack paddy whack,
Give the dog a bone,
This old man came rolling home. } Refrain
This old man, he played two,
He played nick-nack on my shoe.
This old man, he played three,
He played nick-nack on my tree.
This old man, he played four,
He played nick-nack on my door.
This old man, he played five,
He played nick-nack on my hive.
This old man, he played six,
He played nick-nack on my sticks.
This old man he played seven,
He played nick-nack up in heaven.
This old man, he played eight,
He played nick-nack on my gate.
This old man, he played nine,
He played nick-nack on my line.
This old man, he played ten,
He played nick-nack on my hen.

Math
20 MINUTES

Bring the children back to their desks at this point and provide them with small manipulatives for exploration. These may be provided for you in your classroom. They come in many shapes and forms. The children like to use characters that are in the shape of small animals. Give every two children a plain piece of paper that can serve as a counting mat.

Count out a set of ten for counting mat. Place one pipe cleaner on each mat that you have formed into a circle.

Explain to the children that you are giving them ten small counters to play with. Suggest to them that they will take turns. One child may allow as many animals as he wants inside the circle to play and his partner will guess how many are playing. Then, the child who guessed will be the one who allows as many animals as he wants to play and his partner will count how many animals are playing. Next model how to add one more animal to change a total of four to five, etc; and give them time to explore this game.

Lunch

Number the tables by rows and teach each group in turn to join the line silently when you signal it is their turn. Break down this whole procedure into simple sentences suggested by the children and write these sentences on a chart for future reference.

Listening Game
(Who is It?)
10 MINUTES
ORIENTATION
AND
AUDITORY
PERCEPTION

When the children have put away their things from lunch, settle them down by starting work with this quiet game.

Choose someone to hide his eyes in the front of the room- no peeking! Now tap someone on the shoulder to go up to the hidden child and say," Hello." Encourage the speaker to use the name of the hidden child if he knows it. The hidden child can only turn around when the speaker has returned to his seat and everyone says the word, "Ready."

Now the child who was hiding, turns around and faces the class. He is given three guesses to find the speaker. He asks a question like, "Is it Matt?" Whether he guesses who the speaker is or not, the speaker then comes up and hides his eyes and another person is chosen to tap someone to speak. This game helps to improve listening skills and helps the children learn their classmates' names.

Math and Counting
10 MINUTES

Show the children a picture of a bar graph. Explain that a graph can be used to show information clearly. Tell them that today you will ask them to answer a question about the graph that you will make later in the week. Ask the children to think about how they come to school. Do they come by bus? Do they come by train? Do they walk to school?

Next distribute an index card to each child and ask them to write their names on the side with lines on it. Next, show them how to flip over the card and draw a picture of how they come to school. Provide simple instructions for simple illustrations. They can draw themselves as a stick figure and they can draw the car, train or bus with simple shapes. Next collect these cards, making sure you are clear on how they come to school. Tell the children that you will be putting these cards in a safe place so that they can count the ballots later in the week and prepare a graph with you.

Note that it is important that each child has one written ballot because they tend to want to vote more than once. The culmination of this lesson will take place on day three.

Social Studies
20 MINUTES

Introduce the book, *I Am an Apple* by M. Marzella and J. Moffatt. Discuss the stages of an apple's growth from flower bud to fruit. This book provides more than a Science lesson; it provides an example of a sequence of events. You will point out this style of writing many times during the year. At some point you will decide to have the children create their own sequential, "how to" books. An example of this type of book would be, "How to Play Baseball."

Dismissal
20 MINUTES

Begin early. Make certain everyone has all his belongings ready before it is time to leave. Discuss homework with the children. Request that they ask someone in their family to read them a book tonight. This is one of the most valuable things parents can do to help their children learn to read. If you remind the children each day and communicate this goal to their parents early in the year, you will be setting the stage for success in reading.

DAY THREE

Orientation
10 MINUTES

Repeat the procedure of guiding the children into the classroom and settling into their seats. Let the children take turns putting away their belongings. Remind them to take out any notes they may have brought to school and put them in the top corner of their desks.

Next, look around at the children and make eye contact with as many of them as possible. Announce that you will now take the attendance. Remind them of the procedure as explained in Day Two's Script.

Morning Message
20 MINUTES
READING

Gather the children in the Library Area as you did on day two. Settle them by reviewing the finger play, "Open, Shut Them." Open a discussion on the Social Studies topic of transportation. A picture of a school bus or a picture book can serve as a motivation for this discussion. Remind them that they each took a card the previous day and wrote down how they came to school. Review that activity by asking them to raise their hand if they indicated that they came to school by bus, car, train or foot.

Show the children how you have organized their ballots by placing all same votes together with a rubber band. Open up each pack of ballots and count the number of ballots with the children. Place a paper on each pack and write the total number on it.

Tell them that you will be using this information with them tomorrow to make a special Math chart called a graph. Ask them to think about how high each tally will reach when the graph work is completed.

Next bring their attention to this school day and discuss the day, the date and any special event that may be happening in school today. If the children will be working with another teacher during the day, this information might be included in the morning message. Begin writing these simple sentences on an experience chart:

Today is Wednesday

Today is September 10, 2006

Today we will see Miss Sequel

A Word Game

10 MINUTES

Show the children a chart that is standing on an easel or is secured to a wall. This chart should have been prepared beforehand with a few select lines from Script Two's poem, "This Old Man". Read these lines to the children. Have the children read them with you the second time.

Now tell them you have some fun games to play with these words. Next, cover up some words like "drum," "dog" and "home" with sticky notes and see if they can guess what words are missing as you read the poem together.

If you find someone who says, "I can't read," say, "Oh, I think your eyes and your brain are going to surprise you!" Read the poem together slowly and see if volunteers can guess what words are missing as you go along. Coach them to try to make a sensible guess by uncovering the first letter of the word and reminding them to think of a word that rhymes with the last word from the line before. Some might guess the word from memory and that's all right too. Remember to praise them for their efforts. Confidence is the key to learning. After all the words have been uncovered, read and enjoy the poem one more time together before you send the children back to their seats.

After the children are settled in their seats, present the following finger play as a way of retrieving their attention once again.

○   *Here's a ball.*
    Pinch your forefinger and thumb
    together to form a circle.

○   *Here's a ball.*
    Using both hands, bring both forefingers
    and thumbs together to form a circle.

○   *Here's a GREAT big ball!*
    Bring your forefingers together and using
    your arms draw two imaginary curved lines
    that meet at the bottom to form a circle.

Shall we count them?
Are you ready?
One
Make the OK sign
Two
Forefingers and Thumbs together
Three
Draw the imaginary circle.

A Book
Review
20 MINUTES

Hold up the book that you read with the children yesterday entitled, *I Am an Apple.* Use a real apple to demonstrate the words that can describe the apple. Ask them to share with the class what they learned about apples during yesterday's reading. As they offer suggestions, acknowledge them and use a chart paper to write about three or four sentences which contain the word "Apple."

> *Apples grow on a tree.*
> *Apples grow from seeds.*
> *Apples have seeds inside of them*

Through this activity you are reviewing information and you are providing experience in connecting the spoken word with the written word. Read the chart with the children slowly, then quietly, and then in a regular tone of voice. Hang the chart in the classroom. Tell them that you have a special art activity about apples planned for them in the afternoon. When the project is completed you can hang samples of this work near the chart.

Math
20 Minutes

Bring the children back to their desks from the Library Area. After they are settled, explain to them that they are going to have some fun working in a team today. Review the need for cooperation and sharing. Explain who they will be working with and what materials they will be using. Give each team of children a set of cards showing the numbers one through ten. You will have prepared these numbers in advance. Give each team a white paper to serve as a mat and ten small counters and a pipe cleaner twisted into a circle.

Explain how this game is played. One child will show his team member a number and that child will put that many counters on the mat inside the circle. Now the alternate child will show a card for his team member to see and count accordingly. Allow about fifteen minutes for this activity and after a short review ask the children to gather their materials together for collection.

Lunch
20 Minutes

Even though the children are in their third day of school they need patient reminders of what the routine will be and assurance that you will be seeing them very soon. Provide at least twenty minutes before lunch to ensure a smooth transition.

Welcome Back
10 Minutes
Transitional Activity

After the children return from lunch and put their things away you need to provide an activity before jumping into a new lesson. Provide a listening tape of quiet music or children's songs to change the setting from recess to classroom. Play one side of the tape and you will usually see the children become calmer and more ready to focus on learning.

Hand writing
30 Minutes

Provide each child with a piece of lined paper that has been folded into four columns and has one small dot drawn on the top line of each column. Tell the children that this is a special day because they are going to practice their handwriting. Explain that they will be making straight lines today. Look at the alphabet with them and see if they can find letters that are made with at least one straight line. Next have them place their pencil on the first dot in the left column and draw a line down. Encourage them to draw through two spaces and then stop at the next line. Model this on the blackboard. I usually draw a small alligator in the space below and explain that he is very hungry and so he will eat any letter that comes below the line. Its fun and the children don't want to feed the alligator. As with reading, some will not know what to do, some will try, and some will not be ready to do as you suggest. Be patient. Continue the same procedure with the second, third and fourth dot. Next, have them skip a line and guide them to make four more straight lines two spaces long. Place a star or sticker on their work and remember that they have probably tried their best.

An Art Lesson

40 MINUTES

AIM: To Create a Basket with three apples Inside It.

MOTIVATION: Read *Johnny Appleseed* and discuss the story

MATERIALS: A worksheet depicting a basket ✄ four paper apples for each child

PROCEDURE: Explain to the children that they will have three jobs to do today. They will color the basket, color the apples with colors such as red, yellow and green, and glue the apples in the basket, one on top of the other.

CONCLUSION: Follow-up the creation of the basket. Encourage the children to bring in a real apple for a snack tomorrow.

This lesson is an opportunity for the children to review information and sharpen their listening skills. Notice you are giving the children a series of directions for them to remember the order of and carry out in sequence. After the children have completed the projecct, collect each piece and allow it to dry (See Figure 11-27).

Figure 11-27 APPLE BASKET

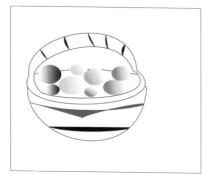

Homework
10 MINUTES

Ask the children to practice writing their straight lines tonight by completing the handwriting exercise started today. Encourage them to ask a family member or friend to read them a story before going to bed.

Dismissal
10 MINUTES

After the collection of the art project, cleanup and discussion of the homework assignments, guide the children to get ready for dismissal. As usual, allow sufficient time to ensure a smooth dismissal.

DAY FOUR

Orientation
10 MINUTES

Follow the routines you have been establishing this week. Make sure they empty their school bags and place them in the closets. Remind them where they should put their lunch boxes and to take out any notes that they brought from home and place them in an upper corner of their desks. Tell them that you will now take the attendance and review what you expect from them. Be mindful that the children have had to deal with a school schedule this week and feeling a little tired. Hopefully a little reassurance will help, as well as a fun learning-day.

Reading
10 MINUTES
ORAL
RECITATION

Gather the children to the meeting area you have established. Compliment them individually for being focused and for being good listeners. Remember to use their names to personalize your comments.

Before you start the morning message try a few finger plays: *Open, Shut Them* (See Page 108), and *Here's a Balloon* below

A Balloon

Now introduce a new finger play:
Here I have a new balloon
Here I have a new balloon

Hold up thumb and forefinger together
Watch me as I blow it

Pinch thumb and forefinger and place them near your lips
Small at first, then bigger, bigger,
Watch it grow and grow

Hold your hand up to form a small balloon and as you speak these words bring your hands away from each other to form a larger and larger balloon.
Do you think it's big enough?
Maybe I should stop!
For if I give another blow
It will surely POP!!

CLAP YOUR HANDS
NOW SAY,
Wasn't that exciting?… But now, I want to see
who can get very quiet and look at me.
Begin to compliment individual children.
I like the way Leah is sitting; I like
the way Janet is looking at me.

Morning Message
15 MINUTES

Turn the children's attention to chart paper and begin a discussion of the day, date and one particular comment about the day. You can write about the weather or something about the book you will read today.

Phonics
30 MINUTES

At this point, send the children back to their seats and when you have their attention, write a letter on the chart paper:

Bb	AIM: To isolate the sound of the letter

Ask the children if they know what letter this is. Ask them if they know a word that begins with that letter. Provide a picture or draw a picture of a bicycle or other object that begins with the letter Bb. Ask for volunteers to suggest words they know that begin with the letter. Write these words in a list:

Bicycle	Ball	Bat	Ban

To isolate the beginning sound further, ask, "Who can come up and circle the b in the word 'bicycle'." Follow this procedure with each of the other words on the list.

Use a small pointer to read each of the words and emphasize the beginning sound.

Ask the children to draw a picture of something that begins with Bb. Help them label their drawings with an appropriate word.

Social Studies
30 MINUTES

On day four you will begin to set up a behavior plan by drawing up positive class rules with your students. Lead the discussion by speaking about what a wonderful school year it will be. Assure the children that you have confidence in them and know that they can work together. As you get their ideas write them in a few simple sentences.

We will work together.
We will be kind.

We will listen in class.

Reread all these sentences and hang this chart in a prominent place for future reference.

Read Aloud
20 MINUTES

For a little comic relief to all this drama about beginning school, I would suggest a book like, *Morris Goes to School* by B. Wiseman. In this book Morris, a moose, makes a series of errors in school because he takes instructions too literally. It will make the children laugh.

After the story, begin getting the children ready for lunch. Follow the procedures you have followed all week.

Math
30 MINUTES

Settle the children into their seats after lunch by using the finger plays introduced this week.

Prepare the skeleton of the bar graph ahead of time by drawing small pictures (🚌) depicting how the children come to school. Draw these pictures along the bottom of the graph.

Bring out the sets of ballots and assist the children in gluing or taping one card above another and on top of the drawing that matches. Now count each pile of cards with the children.

Compare two categories at a time and ask which has more votes. Evaluate the graph as a whole and ask "Which category has the least votes?" and "Which category has the most votes?" "Do any two categories have the same number of votes?"

Place the graph near or in your Math center. Refer to it again for evaluation.

Handwriting
20 MINUTES

Prepare papers for the children as you did for yesterday's lesson. This time you can repeat the exercise in writing the straight line and add a horizontal line on top and one on the bottom of the line to form the capital letter, "I" Remember to reward each attempt with a star or sticker and encourage them to finish practicing this letter for homework.

Homework: Tell the children that you would like them to practice the letter "I" for homework. Guide them to place their handwriting paper in their homework folders.

Encourage them to ask someone in their family or a friend to read them a story.

Dismissal   Assist the children in packing up and getting ready for dismissal. Keep a calm and confident demeanor. Here's where the acting really comes in handy after a long day. Assure them that you will make sure all of them meet the adult who is picking them up. Remind them of their homework. Encourage them to play and rest to get ready for a bright new day tomorrow.

" WELL, SEE YOU TOMORROW, WEATHER PERMITTING, OF COURSE, "

DAY FIVE

Orientation Follow the routines that you are establishing to get the children ready for their day. Now send them slowly to your meeting area to begin the morning message.

Morning Message
10 MINUTES

Today you can emphasize that it is Friday and this is the last day of school before the weekend. Discuss with the children the types of things they like to do on the weekend. For your morning message, include a sentence about the day, one about the date, and a few simple sentences explaining what they like to do on the weekend. Review these sentences before going on to your next activity.

Phonics
10 MINUTES

Review the sound of Bb using yesterday's chart as a reference. If you would like to isolate the initial sound again, you can use a crayon to mark the letters over the circles drawn yesterday. Finally reread all the words with the class. Remember to emphasize this sound as you go through your days. For example, if it is someone's birthday, emphasize the initial sound as you write that word.

Math Through Art
15 MINUTES

Today you will begin to isolate the features of a triangle. You can present the children with something shaped like a triangle or you can simply present them with a colorful drawing or picture of a triangle. Discuss the number of sides and the number of corners a triangle has. Point out the corners or angles. Discuss where we see triangles in our everyday lives. Pizza is always a good example.

Provide the children with a banner shape as described in chapter Two. Prepare these banners ahead of time by writing each individual name with a high lighter. Point out that this triangle has three sides and three angles. Tell them that they are going to make a banner to celebrate our names. We are going to trace our names with a crayon and then add decorations with line designs. Model suggestions and then have the children go ahead and complete their project. Collect these banners and display them in a prominent place.

Social Studies

10 Minutes
Reviewing
a Routine

Practice makes perfect. Choose a routine that you feel your class needs to work on. Maybe this routine might be lining up and walking down the hall. The best way to review a routine is to break it down into simple steps and explain what is expected. Next have a few children help you demonstrate the actions you are expecting. Then involve the whole class in trying to practice the routine effectively. Praise the children for following directions and always expect this cooperation from them. If there is a problem one day, you must start from scratch and review all the steps again. You will be happy that you have invested your time in setting up effective routines because you will be able to spend more and more time teaching and less and less time correcting poor behavior.

Handwriting

30 Minutes

Prepare the worksheets as you have been doing the last few days. Today the children will repeat the straight line and adapt it to make the letter H. Model how the H is made from two vertical lines and one horizontal line. Move slowly, taking time to make each letter as carefully as possible. And, of course, reward their efforts with a sticker, stamp or star.

Tip Toe Train

10 Minutes

Follow the directions on page 110 to provide a transitional activity between this writing activity and lunch. After the game, which should last no more than ten minutes, guide the children to get ready for lunch and remind them of the routines that will take place.

Lunch

See Lunch for Day One, Day Two, Day Three.

Social Studies

30 Minutes

After the children have returned from lunch, you may want to play some quiet music to prepare them for the afternoon activities.

Talk to the children about what a successful week it has been in school. Mention that you have learned so much about them and you are sure they also have learned many things. Ask the children if they have met any new children this week and use this introduction to play the name game again. This time the names can be written on the blackboard with chalk and the children can take turns finding their name and erasing them until no other names remain. Point out the beautiful banners they made today and express how excited you are that visitors, like other teachers, children and their parents, will be admiring them.

Math Review
20 MINUTES

Provide each child with a small round of colored paper with a Popsicle stick attached. Tell the children that today they will have the opportunity to pick one of their favorite numbers (from one to ten) and draw that many happy faces on their "lollipop." You can also suggest other small drawings that you model on the board. Allow the children to take this project home and hang it somewhere in their house. They will be very proud to finish their first week of school and bring home some evidence of their efforts.

Dismissal
20 MINUTES

After the children have gotten their things together, remind them that today is Friday and they will not be coming to school tomorrow or Sunday. Tell them what a wonderful job they have done this week and how you are looking forward to working with them on Monday. For the weekend, their assignment is to play and rest after a long week.

" I HAVE TO GO TO THE SECOND GRADE,
I'M A CAREER WOMAN. "

12

Creating Scripts

"Luck is a matter of preparation meeting opportunity"

–Oprah Winfrey

Soon you will be creating lessons from your curriculum guides and fitting them into your schedule. On the next page, study the sample schedule and use it as you would a menu for the next two weeks. Choose one type of lesson from a selection. Scheduling can be tricky at first but eventually will become second nature. Note that some time has been allowed for flexibility.

Your creativity is boundless when you tap into it. It is this life blood that will infuse your teaching with style. Creativity without planning in any classroom can become chaotic. Begin with the basic lessons and schedules. Follow my scripts to gain a sense of timing in the classroom. Once you have this act down, embellish your days as only you can. Enjoy!

**Warning: Creativity without planning
may become chaotic!**

Schedule

Attendance and Business of the Day		10 MINUTES
Reading Activity / motivation	☐ read aloud ☐ peer reading ☐ a shared reading lesson from reading materials	20 MINUTES
Reading Lesson	☐ a guided reading lesson based on the day's reading activity ☐ creation of a chart ☐ a chart review ☐ review of vocabulary through Word Wall or a activity sheet	20 MINUTES
A Short Recess	Lavatory / possible snack	10 MINUTES
Transitional Activity	☐ Tiptoe Train ☐ The Listening Game ☐ a finger play or poem	10 MINUTES
Math Lesson	☐ number recognition ☐ creation of Sets ☐ introduction of shape ☐ building a sequence	20 MINUTES
Math Activity / Based on Lesson Introduced	☐ hand-on math play ☐ role playing ☐ tracing large numbers or shapes	20 MINUTES

Transitional Activity	☐ movement with quiet music ☐ a quiet game ☐ a read aloud	
Building a Classroom Community	☐ introduction of positive rules ☐ introduction of classroom jobs ☐ introduction of a particular routine ☐ review of any of these lessons	15 MINUTES
An Activity Based on Classroom Community Lesson	☐ creating and reviewing a classroom chart ☐ brainstorming which jobs need to be done in the classroom ☐ a simulation of a particular job	
Preparation for Lunch	☐ classroom discussion followed by orderly procedures ☐ lunch	
Transitional Activity (Choose one not yet used today)	☐ Tiptoe Train ☐ The Listening Game ☐ a Finger play or poem	10 MINUTES
Handwriting	*Provide children with lined paper. Model the formation and spacing of one of the following and allow time for trial and error* ☐ a straight line ☐ a capital L ☐ a capital F ☐ a capital E ☐ a capital I	20 MINUTES

Orientation: An Art Lesson	*Introduce one of the activities with a discussion. Provide a model of at least one finished product.* ☐ drawing a self portrait ☐ drawing a family picture ☐ creating a page for a booklet entitled, "All About Me"	30 MINUTES
A Day's Review	*Conclude the day by discussing what was learned today. Review any homework assignments for this evening. Slowly prepare for dismissal.*	20 MINUTES

Weaving your lessons together

The philosophy of holistic education holds that when studying one subject, you are utilizing skills and informaltion from other subjects. Remember the voting activities explained in the initial scripted lessons? This Social Studies topic utilized the Math concepts of counting and comparing. A graphic bar graph was completed to provide a picture of the voting results. These activities added breadth and depth to a discussion of voting. This experience became a reference point for these children when they noticed that their parents were voting on Election Day. Although the children's experience was much more simplified than their parents, the basic concept was communicated.

Brainstorming

Given any topic, you can come up with some activities that will immerse the children in learning. Practice doing this with a few topics in your curriculum guides before looking at the ones suggested in your teacher's guides. Join with colleagues to brainstorm together. You will be surprised at all the ideas that will be generated. Young children have trouble understanding time. Studying the seasons can help them to notice time passing. Of course, if you are in an area that does not experience all four seasons, you may focus more on the passing of the months of the year.

Generating activities for the Fall

- Collect Fall leaves for display in the classroom.
- Trace a leaf on a piece of colored paper.
- Teach the names of the different types of leaves.
- Categorize your collection of leaves by type.
- Use the leaves to decorate a self portrait of each child.
- Create a Fall wreath. Use a paper plate with a circle cut from it for the base.
- Make a mobile of Fall leaves. Use a hanger and tie strings of colored yarn on it to attach leaves.
- Trace and cut leaves from colored tissue paper.
- Tape tissue paper leaves on the windows.
- Count all the leaves the children have collected to find a total number.
- Count how many of each type of leaf were found.
- Compare sets of leaves to determine which sets have more or less.
- Graph your findings on a bar graph.
- Name the colors you see on the leaves.
- Mix colors to create new colors by adding food coloring to cups of water.
- Read a poem about Fall.
- Display this poem in your classroom.
- Create an Acrostic poem about the Fall with your class.
- Make a class collage using different leaves or cut-outs. Add class photos.
- Use colored leaf cut-outs to create patterns with your class.
- Read fiction and non-fiction books about leaves.
- Use the computer to search for more information.
- Have the children draw pictures about the season.
- Combine the children's pictures to create a class booklet.
- Take a walk to observe nature.
- Collect acorns that have fallen from trees.
- Start a unit on seeds
- Have a Fall celebration. Celebrate the children's work. Invite the parents.

Some teachers prefer to rely on curriculum guides to plan their days, weeks and months. There is nothing wrong with that. It will take confidence to waiver from the rote lessons and units that are presented to you. Ad-libbing will only work for you when you are ready. You will know it is time to try new ideas when you feel your confidence building in yourself and in your students. At that point, allow a time period in your schedule for a more open ended activity. The results can be exciting!

13

Conflicts on the set

"All children are gifted. Some just open their presents later than others"
–Unknown

Children will come into your class with their own strengths and weaknesses. It will be your job to recognize these traits. As a director you will need to understand each child and channel him or her down the road to learning. It is necessary that you come from a place of confidence and strength in order to deal with conflicts on the set effectively. This can be a challenge if you really are not sure how to turn a conflict around. This chapter will deal directly with specific conflicts that you may encounter during the first few days of school. Each scene will present you with a specific challenge you might face and give you directions for how to deal with it.

Each solution takes into account the possible needs of the child at that time and what he or she might need from you in order to conform. With skillful understanding you will have a good chance of refocusing the child on the school scenario. Read this chapter before the first day of school and refer to it when you need to prevent or resolve a conflict. This information may prove to be invaluable.

Picture this: Weeping Will

It begins with a low whine that can erupt into a loud wail. Chances are that this child does not want to be in school right now. Maybe it is the excitement of a new environment; it might be that he would just rather be at home. It may take time to work it all out, but you need to deal with Weeping Will today. In fact, you need to deal with him right now.

Your first goal should be to take charge but this will not happen without some work on your part. Demanding that he stop will probably make him cry even louder. Take a moment to think before you speak. Think about this child and what his world has been like so far today. If this is your first experience teaching, you may be feeling some anxiety too. Think about the approach that you might want someone to take with you in order to make you feel a little better. Now you are ready to direct.

Act One-Scene One

- Walk over to this child and stoop down so that you are looking at him eye to eye. Hopefully you are feeling compassion at this time but if not, act compassionately.

- Introduce yourself to him and quietly ask him what the problem is. Ask him to tell you more about what is on his mind.

- Echo what he is telling you to assure him that he is being heard.

- Offer him a tissue. Offer him a seat near you. Assure him that you have a wonderful day planned in this brand new classroom.

- Tell the children that you understand what Will might be feeling and share your own feelings of excitement about meeting all of them today.

- Enlist the support of the children to befriend Will during the day.

When Will perceives you as a non-threatening person, it may give him the security to stop weeping. Now he will have a chance to refocus on his new learning environment. By handling this conflict successfully, you have gained respect from Will and from the other students in the class.

Picture this: **Stubborn Sam**

Sam walks into the classroom with the other children, but his body language suggests that he is not a happy camper. His feet are planted firmly where he is standing and he is looking at you with an angry scowl. You invite him to sit but he refuses and you are starting to feel intimidated. The other children have noticed Sam and some of them seem intimidated, too. Now they are looking at you. There is an uneasy feeling in the air. A crisis is looming. You must change the scene, but how?

Act two-Scene One

Before you can begin to change this scene, you must get into character. You must seem sure that you can turn this situation around. You must show no doubt. After you have seated all the other children, turn to Sam.

- Invite him to sit down in a calm but firm voice.

- If he refuses, repeat your request as if it is the first time you delivered this line.

- If he speaks rudely or uses any foul language, tell him that this language is not acceptable in this classroom. Stay in control; don't react emotionally.

- Now give him this choice: Tell him that he is welcome to stand for a while but the seat is there for him when he is ready to sit.

- Move to a position in the front of the room and begin your morning routines.

Many times by moving the spotlight away from a stubborn child, you are relieving his need to act out. I have seen children stand for a minute or two and then silently sit down as all eyes are fixed on me. By refusing to show him any sign of intimidation you will succeed and win the respect of your students.

Picture this: Ali B. Me

You begin your lesson and you hear Ali call out, "I know that all ready!" You ask for volunteers and Ali always wants to be chosen. You try to allow time for a shy child to speak and Ali answers for her. What's this character all about and how can you work with her?

Chances are Ali is seeking to be noticed. She seeks your attention at any cost. She is ready to be a star student but doesn't notice the other stars around her. She's unsure of how she can get your attention. She tries in both positive and negative ways.

If you notice that there is someone in the class like this, make a note that you will need to plan some lessons on cooperation in group activities. These lessons will help Ali become more aware of the other children in the class. Ali's strengths will be channeled in such a way that she becomes an asset to the other children. Right now, it may be difficult for you to appreciate those strengths.

Act Three - Scene One

- Thank Ali for sharing but ask her not to call out, since it is important to hear the other children's ideas, too.

- When it is time for Ali to offer an idea, show appreciation for what she has to say. Ask her another question about her opinion.

- Tell Ali that you are planning to choose her for a monitor job early on. She can interpret this by concluding that you do notice her talents.

- Always appreciate her input but insist on your initial request not to call out. Be consistent.

By channeling Ali's strengths you are not only helping her immensely, you are affecting the children around her. You are beginning to change a group of individual students into a unified cooperative cast. Congratulations to you!

Picture this: Leo Lost

Leo Lost can't find his pencil. He can't find his book. Oh, and that note his Mother asked him to give you, he can't find that either. He's looking unsettled and things don't seem quite right. He suggests that he get a pencil from his brother who is in a classroom down the hall.

Keep in mind that Leo is still a child. He has come to school to learn how to be a student. He will need your support to gain organizational skills. You will need to set up communication between the school and the home. Hopefully in time, with your guidance, Leo's organizational skills will improve. But as in the previous scenes, the question is, what can you do now?

Act Four - Scene One

- Reassure Leo that you have a pencil for him and give it to him immediately.

- If he has not brought any other supplies with him today reassure him that you will provide him with anything he needs.

- Suggest to Leo that he might want to choose someone from the class who he can depend on during the day. This will help ensure that he doesn't get lost within the school.

- Have him choose someone who he feels comfortable relying on.

- Pay attention to the parent note that Leo said he cannot seem to find. When you get some time, try to reach the parents by phone to hear their concerns.

- Talk to Leo often during the day so he understands that he is an important member of the classroom.

- Assist Leo in packing and unpacking his school bag from day to day until he understands what is expected of him.

In time you will probably notice that Leo is becoming more responsible. Your understanding and guidance are essential to causing this character transformation. You will always remember the positive effect you had on Leo in this, your brand new classroom.

Picture this: Silly Jill

The children are all seated at their desks and you are ready to begin a lesson. You notice that Jill is looking inside her desk instead of looking up at you. You walk near her desk and see that Jill is playing with a small toy she has brought from home. She doesn't seem interested in you or your lesson; she would rather play.

You need to bring Jill's attention to the lesson at hand and motivate her to get more involved with school and less involved with her toy. You want to accomplish this goal without causing a scene and you need some suggestions.

Act Five - Scene One

- Try not to show negative emotions about the situation. Her lack of attention has nothing to do with you.

- Tell Jill that you notice that she is playing with a toy and you would like her to place the toy in her school bag until later on.

- Assure her that you have some fun activities planned for this very special first day of school.

- If she puts it away, thank her and tell her that you know she will enjoy playing with the toy after school.

- If she refuses to put the toy in the school bag, don't insist. Suggest an alternative to her. She can put the toy in her school bag or she can place it all the way in the back of her desk so that it can rest there until later.

By handling the situation this way, you are allowing Jill to make a choice. That is most important. Jill needs to draw the conclusion that learning can be just as fun as playing with toys. It will be your expertise as a brand new teacher that will lead her to that point.

Children can be a challenge to work with but with skillful directing you can refocus their attention. By treating each of them with patience and understanding, and by following my suggestions, you will be starting a successful school year!

14

Scripted questioning techniques

"Some books are to be tasted; others swallowed;
and some to be chewed and digested"

—Francis Bacon

There will be many opportunities in the lower grades for discussion. You, as the director, will facilitate learning through discussions of children's literature. I have developed these scripted questions from studying Bloom's Taxonomy. Thinking about levels of thinking skills can guide you to become adept in leading the children to think beyond a simple knowledge question and to delve into deeper analysis of the story. Your questioning will need to be more sophisticated than ones with obvious answers.

If you insist that a friend watch the latest hit movie, that you have already seen, you may begin to give a quick synopsis of the plot. As you rattle off the beginning, jump to the middle and rush to the end of the movie, you are helping your friend to understand the whole plot. After you have his attention, he may start to ask you more detailed questions about the movie. He may do this to help clarify what he has heard or to help him to visualize the movie more clearly. As you respond, you are helping him to put all the pieces of the puzzle together before he decides that this is a movie he would like to see.

Think of this analogy as you creating **comprehension** and **knowledge** questions about the picture book you read to your class. You want your students to understand the main parts of the story you are reading. They have listened to the story carefully if they can tell you more details about the characters and storyline, too. Examples of comprehension and knowledge questions can be found in the charts that follow in this chapter.

After seeing a movie, you may discuss it. You might begin a discussion by putting yourself in one of the character's places and either agreeing or disagreeing with one of her decisions within the movie. Or, you use one of the lines from the dialogue to demonstrate the impact of this idea on you. You are using the skill of **application**. Sometimes this activity serves to clarify parts of the movie for someone in the group. "Oh, that's why he did that. Now I get it." This discussion allows you to jump into the character's skin and then jump back and react in your own way. In the classroom setting, children can be asked to role play a part of a book in order to better understand an important scene or a series of related scenes. You ask your students to react to the story they have heard by making a picture of one scene and a sentence or two about what went on. All of this activity relates to the application question.

The discussion can get intense as you delve into the whys of the movie. Innuendos of the story need to be explored. You and your friends begin your search by **analyzing** the question, "why" as it relates to all that has gone on in the movie. What feelings did the director really want to get across? What were the clues that make you believe that intention? Think of using a magnifying glass and studying the clues of the story when you create your analysis questions.

Synthesis is the process of taking parts of something and understanding them as a whole. With this understanding you can progress one step beyond analysis. Suppose you produce and direct a sequel to the movie you have seen. You make changes to the plot and characterization in your new movie. You have moved beyond your understanding of the first movie to create something new in the second movie.

Challenging your students to think beyond what they have heard is the basis of synthesis. Note the various synthesis questions in the charts further in this chapter. Each one challenges the student to create something new after he has reviewed the picture book read for comprehension.

We are all familiar with **evaluations**. Here we pass judgment on what we have heard and seen. Evaluations are done at the time of an awards ceremony. "Best, second best. Thank you to everyone who has made this possible!" In the classroom setting, we ask the children to judge what they have read during a read aloud or shared reading experience. When we ask the children what they thought of the book, children have a tendency to answer with short simple answers. It is our job as a facilitator of a discussion to guide them to share a little more information about their evaluation. And so we might ask questions like, "Would you recommend this book to a friend? Why or why not?" In order to help your young students to get in touch with their feelings and make an evaluation, you ask a question like, "If you could show how your face looked when you left the movie theatre, how would it look? Did you say anything about the movie when you left the theatre? Can you share that with us?" This prompt helps young children to think back and remember an experience and match it with a feeling. We want students to be aware that they can express their individual feelings through a personal evaluation.

Later on in this chapter you will find sets of questions for some picture books. After reading one of the books simply ask the questions I suggest. You will feel you are acting like an experienced teacher without having to put in much preparation. You will enjoy the results!

You may want to use the following suggestions to create a set of questions for a particular story. Need more help...study the ready-made sets of questions that follow

It's a Question of .....

Comprehension Ask a question about the key points of the story. Ask how to tell how a problem arose in the story. Ask how the issue was resolved.

Knowledge Ask a question about obvious details! Ask someone to recall a name or place for an event in the story.

Application Ask your students to tell how they would act in a similar situation. Ask them to role play a scene from the story. Ask them to write or draw about the story.

Analysis Ask them to think beyond the obvious facts. Ask them to consider why a character acted in a certain way. Why did the story end the way it did?

Synthesis Take it one step further. Ask them to create a new idea: a new ending or change within the story. Ask them to invent something based on the story.

Evaluation Ask them what they think of the book. Would they recommend it to their friend? Why or why not?

The Polar Express
Written and illustrated by Chris Van Allsburg

Name three ways the boys celebrated when they were on the train.	Knowledge
Can you remember what animals were in the forest?	Comprehension
How can we compare the trip on a mountain to a roller coaster?	Comprehension
What happened at the beginning of the story?	Comprehension
What happened in the middle of the story?	Comprehension
How did the story end?	Comprehension
Why did the conductor use a pocket watch and look up at the boy's window?	Analysis
If we interview the boy about his trip what could we ask him?	Analysis
What would you want to change about the story?	Synthesis
Would you recommend this story to a friend? Why or why not?	Evaluation

Stellaluna
Janell Cannon

At what time of day did Stellaluna and her baby search for food?	Knowledge
Describe how some baby birds helped Stellaluna stay alive when she lost her mother?	Comprehension
What other animals in the story could have helped Stellaluna?	Analysis
What did Stellaluna teach the baby birds that turned out to be dangerous for them?	Knowledge
How do you think Stellaluna felt being different from the birds?	Evaluation
What type animal was Stellaluna?	Comprehension
Can you think of another story we have read in which the character feels he is different from the others in the story?	Analysis
What happened at the end of the story to make things better for Stellaluna?	Evaluation
Let's find more books about birds and then we can compare bird habits with bat habits.	Application

Where the Wild Things Are
Maurice Sendak

What was Max's punishment for getting into trouble?	Knowledge
Can you explain how Max traveled to the land of the Wild?	Comprehension
How long did it take Max to get to the destination?	Knowledge
What questions would you ask the "Wild Things?"	Application
Why do you think Max wanted to give the "Wild Things" orders to start a rumpus?	Analysis
Can you think of a game you can make up to play with the "Wild Things?"	Synthesis
What do you think Max's mother was feeling when she left Max's supper in his room for him at the end of the story?	Evaluation

A Busy Year
Leo Lionni

In what month did the mice meet Woody the Tree?	Knowledge
What month came after that in the story?	Knowledge
Describe the conversation the mice had with Woody?	Comprehension
What do you like to talk about with your friends?	Application
Let's make a seasonal clock showing the 4 different seasons described in the book	Application
Were the mice good friends to Woody? Why or why not?	Evaluation
Can you help me list all the months of the year on a chart?	Application

Swimmy
Leo Lionni

Tell how Swimmy got lost in the ocean?	Knowledge
List the things that Swimmy saw while swimming in the ocean. You can use words or pictures for your answer.	Knowledge
How did Swimmy's life change when he met the school of fish?	Comprehension
How did the fish learn to work together so they wouldn't be eaten by the bigger fish?	Comprehension
Here are six templates of large fish. Let's take turns sharing them and tracing the templates Inside the fish you have drawn, you can draw all the little fish with the red crayon. When you are finished you can draw Swimmy, the little black fish, with your black crayon.	Application
Why do you think the fish were stronger when then swam together?	Evaluation
Note: A simple fish template can be made on tag board or cardboard by drawing a long large oval and a smaller triangle for the tail.	

Peter's Chair
Ezra Jack Keats

What did Peter use to make his building?	Knowledge
Tell why Peter's mother asked him to play quietly	Knowledge
Describe how you think Peter was feeling when he saw his new baby sister resting in the cradle?	Comprehension
Why do think Peter's dad asked him to help paint the old high chair?	Comprehension
What things did Peter do to get away from the new baby and his parents?	Knowledge
Draw a picture of a boy about Peter's age. We can draw him like a stick man. Next let's draw the baby's crib and high chair.	Application
Can Peter use the crib or highchair anymore? Why or why not?	Evaluation
Turn your paper over again. This time draw furniture that Peter can use now.	Synthesis
After reading this whole story, can you guess why Peter changed his mind about getting the smaller furniture ready for his sister?	Evaluation

Madeline
Ludwig Bemelmans

Describe Madeline and how she dressed.	Knowledge
What happed to Madeline that caused her to go to the hospital?	Knowledge
How did the girls walk on line in the hall? Did they always have partners?	Knowledge
Do you walk on line in the hall in the same way?	Analysis
Let's role play. Let's pretend we are Madeline's class and get on line like they do.	Application
Let's make a get-well card for Madeline. What can we draw on the front of it?	Synthesis
Do you think Miss Clavel was a kind person?	Evaluation

The Quilt Story
Tony Johnston and Tomie DePaola

What did Abigail's mom sew on her quilt?	Knowledge
Where and when did Abigail live?	Knowledge
Let's made a diorama (3-dimensional picture within a box) together showing the inside of the house that you live in.	Synthesis
Later in the story when Abigail put the quilt in the attic, it became a home for some animals. Can you name the animals that lived in the quilt?	Knowledge

Now One Foot, Now the Other
Story and Pictures by Tomi DePaola

What was the first word Bobby said?	Knowledge
Who also had this name in the family?	Knowledge
Describe the blocks that Bobby and his father played with together.	Comprehenson
Can two volunteers show us how Bobby's grandfather taught him how to walk?	Application
If you could teach your classmates how to play a game of catch, what would you tell them to do first? What are the next steps they would have to take?	Synthesis
Explain how Bobby helped his grandfather get better after he became sick.	Comprehension

Miss Nelson has a Field Day
James Marshall, Harry Allard

Describe how the people in the school were feeling at the beginning of the story.	Knowledge
What team will the school's football team play next?	Knowledge
Why do you think Coach Armstrong was feeling so bad?	Comprehension
Describe how Miss Nelson helped the team out.	Analysis
Let's make some signs we could hold up if we were going to the football game.	Synthesis
Would you recommend this story to your friends? Why or why not?	Evaluation

Conclusion

*"Consider the postage stamp: Its usefullness
consists in the ability to stick to one thing
till it gets there."*

—Josh Billings

You have brought so much to the teaching profession. Besides your degree you have brought all your talents and gifts to the table. Only you will decide what approaches you would like to adopt. You will interpret what you have learned and present your lessons as only you can. Ideas are just that. You will choose which ones work for you and incorporate them. As you gain experience, your confidence will grow. It is this confidence that will lead you to success.

Since I have used the stage as a metaphor, I will conclude by suggesting that you can liken this theory to one found in a classic movie, the Wizard of Oz. Dorothy felt she needed to find the wizard so that she could travel home to Kansas. The tin man, the lion and the scarecrow joined her so they could seek their own personal goals. Well, they found the wizard, but soon disappointment set in. They discovered that the Wizard was not as powerful as they had hoped. After recovering from their shock and disappointment they realized that he probably would not be magically able to grant any of their wishes! But that was not the end of the story. He gave each of Dorothy's friends a token of their hearts' desires so they could feel like they had actually been granted their request. For Dorothy his advice was clear. He told her that she always had the power to go back to Kansas. She just had to believe she did. And so when Dorothy had lost all hope of the wizard bringing her home, she closed her eyes and clicked her heels and sent herself back home. My point is this. You have the power to be a successful teacher. Despite the challenges that you will face, you will be able to succeed. What you need is that same confidence that Dorothy had and my hope is that this book will provide that for you.

Teaching has many beginnings. You will begin every September with a brand new set of children. Keep this book handy. It will remind you of what you need to do to start and it will provide you with time to use for more and more of your creative ideas. Thank you for choosing teaching. I hope many children and parents thank you throughout your career. You have chosen a profession of hope: hope in our children, hope in their futures and hope in our world. And remember, you are just the one for this job and you'll do great!

Appendix

Appendix A
Children's Literature

The Very Hungary Caterpillar
by Eric Carle
Philomel Books

Johnny Appleseed
by Stephen Kellogg
Harper, Collins, 1988

I am Me
by Alexa Brandenberg
Harcourt Brace & Company

Corduroy
by Don Freeman
Viking

Red Leaf, Yellow Leaf
by Louis Ehlert
Harcourt, Brace & Company

Number One Number Fun
by Kay Charao
Holiday House

Mathew's Dream
by Leo Lionni
Alfred A. Knopf

Anno's Counting Book
by Milsumoso Anno
Thomas Y. Crowell, 1975

Harry the Dirty Dog
by Gene Lion
Illustrated by Margaret Graham;

Morris Goes to School
by B. Wiseman
Harper Trophy, 1983

I am Apple
(Hello Reader! Science Level I)
by Jean Marzollo & Judith Marzollo

Do You Want to be My Friend
by Eric Carle
Harper, Collins

Clifford Goes to School
by Norman Bridell
Scholastic Press

Counting Penquins Zero to Nine
by Caroline Walton How
Harper's Row

The Carrot Seed
by Gene Lion
Illustrated by Crockett Johnson
Harper, Collins

Ten Little Bears: A Counting Rhyme
by Kathleen Hague
Illustrated by Michael Hague
Morroe Junior Books, 1999

A Color of His Own
by Leo Lionni
Pantheon Books

Where the Wild Things Are
by Maurice Sendak
Houghton Mifflin

Appendix A (Contiued)
Children's Literature

A Busy Year
by Leo Lionni
Alfred A. Knopf

Swimmy
by Leo Lionni
Pantheon, 1968

Peter's Chair
by Ezra Jack Keats
Harper Row

Madeline
by Ludig Bemelmans
Viking Press

The Quilt Story
by Tony Johnson & Tommie DePaola
G. P. Putnam & Sons

Miss Spider's ABC's
by David Kirk
Scholastic Press

Now One Foot, Now the Other
by Tommie DePaola
G. P. Putnam & Sons

The Polar Express
by Chris Van Allsburg
Houghton Mifflin

Miss Nelson Has a Field Day
by James Marshall & Harry Allard
Houghton Mifflin

Appendix B

Dolch Words

And	Every	She	Into	We
If	May	Call	Down	Wash
Away	Us	Cut	With	Much
Here	My	It	Or	As
Tell	Any	Brown	Went	Just
Know	Goes	Then	Not	Will
Come	Help	Read	Always	Because
Could	Better	Run	Are	Burt
Work	Those	Got	Sing	In
Who	Around	Find	Grow	Your
This	Wish	At	Jump	Was
Put	To	Four	Buy	Let
Funny	Done	Thank	Would	Is
Round	Laugh	Do	Very	Once
He	Off	Go	Only	Up
Never	Both	There	So	What
Open	Pretty	For	Came	Over
Please	From	Keep	Kind	Try
Before	Not	Our	Draw	Fast
Pull	About	Small	Fly	Far
Had	On	Full	Can	An
Carry	See	Start	Ask	Must
Right	How	Saw	His	Some
Own	Sleep	Bring	Said	Six
Cold	Say	Were	Two	Red
Take	Yes	Does	Be	When
Black	Green	Show	Like	Him
Write	Now	Her	I	Big
Me	The	Is	Has	Soon
By	Many	Did	Ran	Together
That	Again	Old	A	Eat
Don't	Good	Eight	One	Upon
Ride	After	While	These	They
Thank	Out	Made	Their	Which
Under	Too	Want	Make	Myself
Look	Blue	Long	Sit	Live
Today	Grave	Walk	Ate	You
Have	First	Play	Warm	Pick
Little	Use	No	Fall	All

Appendix B (Continued)

Dolch Words

But	Light
Am	Going
Yellow	Been
Of	Ten
Get	Hold
Seven	Give
New	Where
Stop	Best
Three	Shall
Drink	
Why	
Clean	
Five	
Them	

Appendix C
Bibliography

Assertive Discipline: A Take Charge Approach for Today's Educator
by Lee Canter
Lee Canter & Associates, Santa Monica CA
ISBN: 0-9608978-0-1

Lee Canter's Assertive Discipline Elementary Workbook Grades K to 5
by Lee Canter
Lee Canter & Associates, Santa Monica CA

Acting Lessons for Teachers: Using Performance Skills in the Classroom
by Robert Tauber & Cathy Sargent Mester
Praeger, Westport CT

Acting Games: Improvisatons and Exercises
by Marsh Cassady
Meriwether Publishing LTD
ISBN: 0-916260-92-5

The Art of Teaching Reading
by Lucy McCormick Calkins
Pearson Education, 2000

Guided Reading: Good First Teaching for All Children
by Gay Sue Pinnell & Irene E. Fauntas
Heineman, 1996

The Absorbent Mind
by Maria Montessori
OWI Books, NY

Dr. Montessori's Own Handbook
by Maria Montessori & Nancy McCormick Rambush
Schnocken Books, 1988

Literature In Bloom: A Whole Language Approach to Literature
Enhanced
By Bloom's Taxonomy
By Molly Lyle & Pamela Treadwell
LinquiSystems, Inc., 1990

Appendix C

Bibliography

Software

Accelerated Reader
for K to 3
Renassance Learning Inc
PO Box 8036
Wisconsin Rapids, Wisconsin 54495-8036
(866) 846-7323

Jump Start Phonics
(K to 3)
www.adventure.com
(800) 725-9707

Reader Rabbitt
(K to 3)
Learning Company
100 Pine Street, Suite 1900
San Franscisco
www.borderbund.com
(415) 659-2000

Math Blaster
(K to 3)
www.adventure.com
(800) 871-2969

Videos

Phonics for the First Grade
Carson-Dellosa Publishing Co., Inc
PO Box 35665
Greensboro NC 27425
www.carsondellosa.com
(336)-632-0084

Appendix C
Bibliography

Resources on the Internet for Early Grade Teachers

Education Place
What I like about this site is that you can create a monthly theme for your classroom. Just click on Monthly themes on the left side of the site to find out about it.
http://eduplace.com

Sites for Teachers
Hundreds of site links are listed. Each link gives a brief description of what the site is about.
http://sitesforteachers.com

SBC Knowledge Network Explorer
It's a great place to search. If you are looking for a lesson plans, just check early grades and choose lesson plans. You can find anything from craft activities to tools here
http://kn.pacbell.com/wired/bluewebn

Discovery
Excellent lesson planning resources.
http://school.discovery.com

Scholastic
Scholastic has a sight for resources with early grade teachers in mind.
http://teacher.scholastic.com

Appendix D

Figure List & Association

Figure	Page	Association
Class List 3-1	39	Organization
Name Plaques 3-2	39	Organization & Recognition
Monitor Chart 3-3	40	Recognition & Motivation
Name Banner 3-4	42	Identity
Acrostic Poem 3-5	42	Social Skills
'Initial' Collage 3-6	42	Identity & Creativity
Classroom Map 4-7	46	Organization
Supply List 4-8	48	Organization
Parent Letter 4-9	49	Identity & Organization
Color Wheel 6-10	59	Creativity, Mood
Note Holder 7-11	67	Creativity & Identity
Seasonal Hat 7-12	67	Creativity & Identity
Boxes / Baskets 7-13	67	Creativity & Math & Identity
Collage 7-14	67	Creativity & Identity
Spots 7-15	70	Math & Spatial Awareness
Rainbow Plate 7-16	70	Creativity & Identity
Windsock 7-17	70	Creativity & Identity
Door Hanger 7-18	70	Identity & Parent Involvement
Chunk Shapes 7-19	73	Math & Spatial Awareness
Recipe 8-20	80	Math & Spatial Awareness
Stop Germs 9-21	88	Lesson Plan Creation
Rounds 10-22	94	Identity
Reminder Chart 10-23	94	Organization & Math
Calendar Story 10-24	95	Sense of Timing
Shapes 10-25	95	Reasoning & Math
Seasonal Chart 10-26	97	Sense of Timing
Apple Basket 10-27	122	Creativity & Identity

Appendix E
About the Author

Carol Keeney has thirty-three years experience teaching early childhood grades. Many years were spent as a first grade teacher in the New York City school system. While tenured with the school system, Carol helped develop a science curriculum at the request of her school district.

Carol spent many years as an adjunct professor at the College of New Rochelle in New York, and while tenured, has critiqued peer professors at the request of the college. She is currently working as an Adjunct Professor at Norwalk Community College in Norwalk, Connecticut.

Carol holds an MS degree in Education from St. John's University. She was nominated and listed in the *Who's Who of American Teachers*.

Carol has developed and taught many courses. Her favorites are Methods of Teaching Early Childhood Education, Methods of Teaching Reading to Normal and Special Children and Methods of Teaching Creative Arts in the Classroom.

Index

Index **173**

W

Words 91
  Dolch 55
  how words work 41
  phonics 55, 124, 127
  This Old Man 118
  Word Game 113
  word wall 54